DARWIN
A GRAPHIC BIOGRAPHY

THE REALLY EXCITING
AND DRAMATIC STORY
OF A MAN WHO
MOSTLY STAYED AT HOME
AND
WROTE SOME BOOKS

By EUGENE BYRNE AND SIMON GURR

✸ Smithsonian Books

WASHINGTON, DC

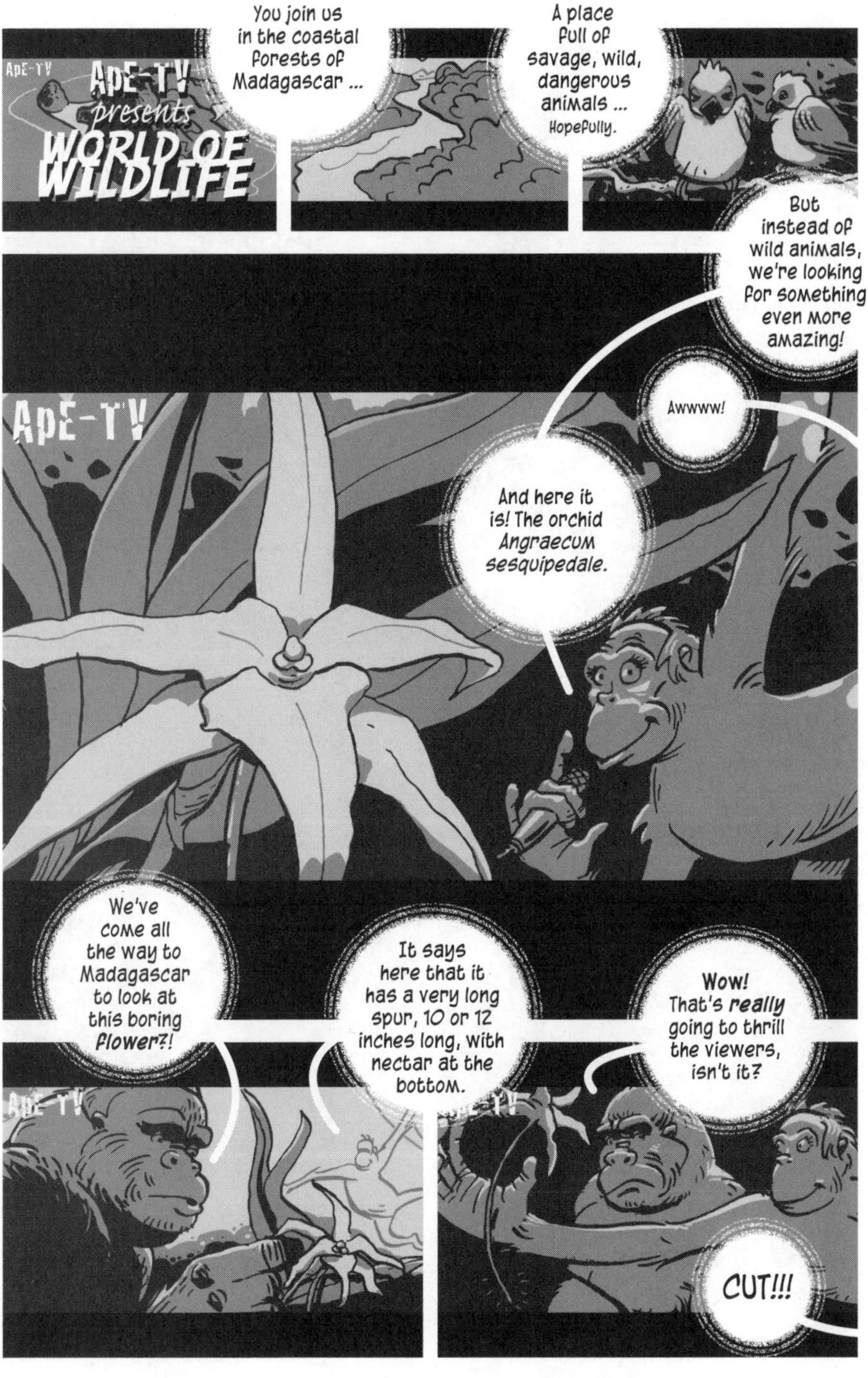
ApE-TV
ApE-TV presents WORLD OF WILDLIFE
You join us in the coastal forests of Madagascar ...
A place full of savage, wild, dangerous animals ...
Hopefully.
But instead of wild animals, we're looking for something even more amazing!
ApE-TV
Awwww!
And here it is! The orchid *Angraecum sesquipedale.*
We've come all the way to Madagascar to look at this boring *flower*?!
It says here that it has a very long spur, 10 or 12 inches long, with nectar at the bottom.
ApE-TV
Wow! That's ***really*** going to thrill the viewers, isn't it?
CUT!!!

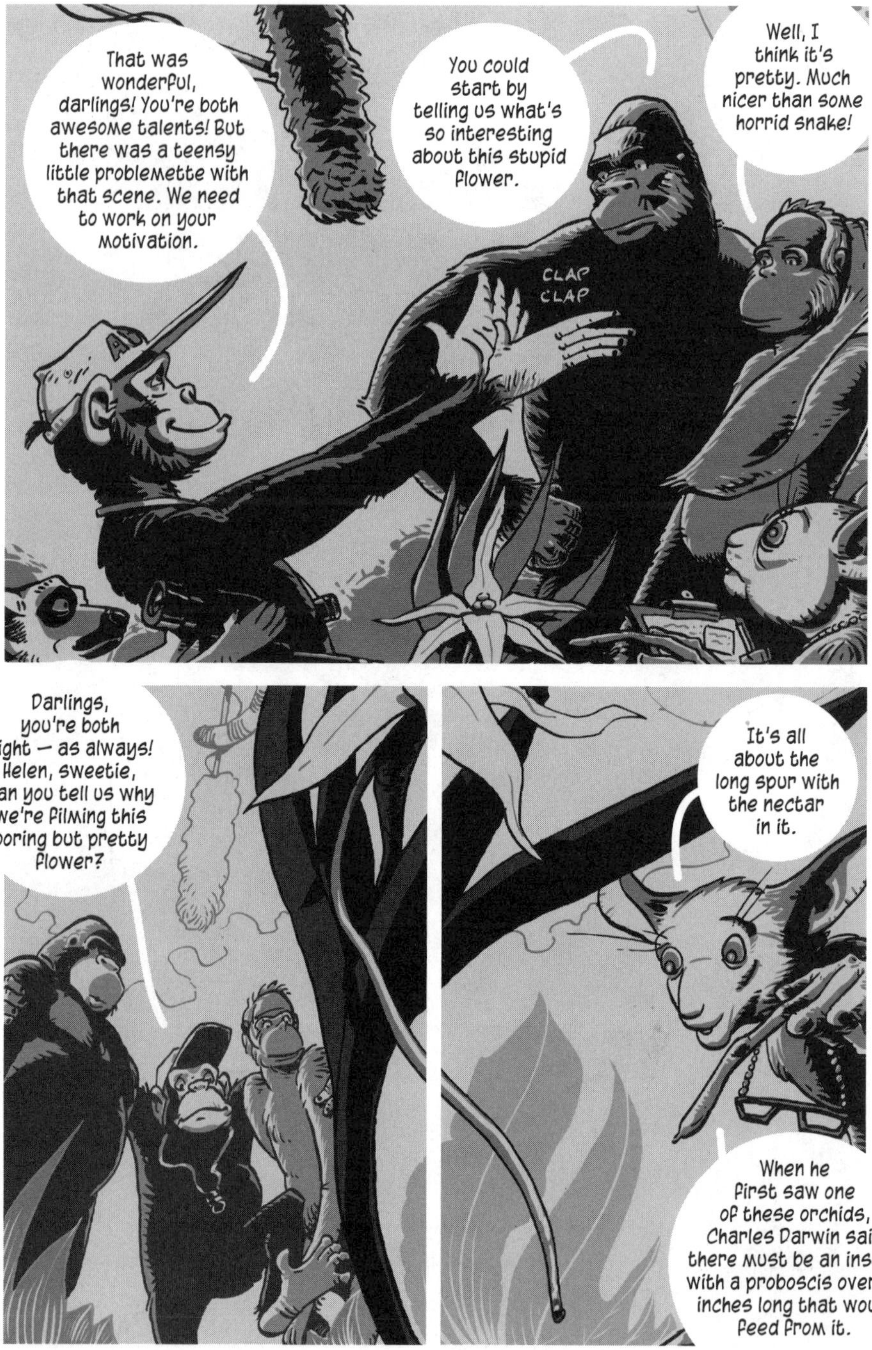

That was wonderful, darlings! You're both awesome talents! But there was a teensy little problemette with that scene. We need to work on your motivation.
You could start by telling us what's so interesting about this stupid flower.
Well, I think it's pretty. Much nicer than some horrid snake!
CLAP CLAP
Darlings, you're both right — as always! Helen, sweetie, can you tell us why we're filming this boring but pretty flower?
It's all about the long spur with the nectar in it.
When he first saw one of these orchids, Charles Darwin said there must be an insect with a proboscis over 10 inches long that would feed from it.

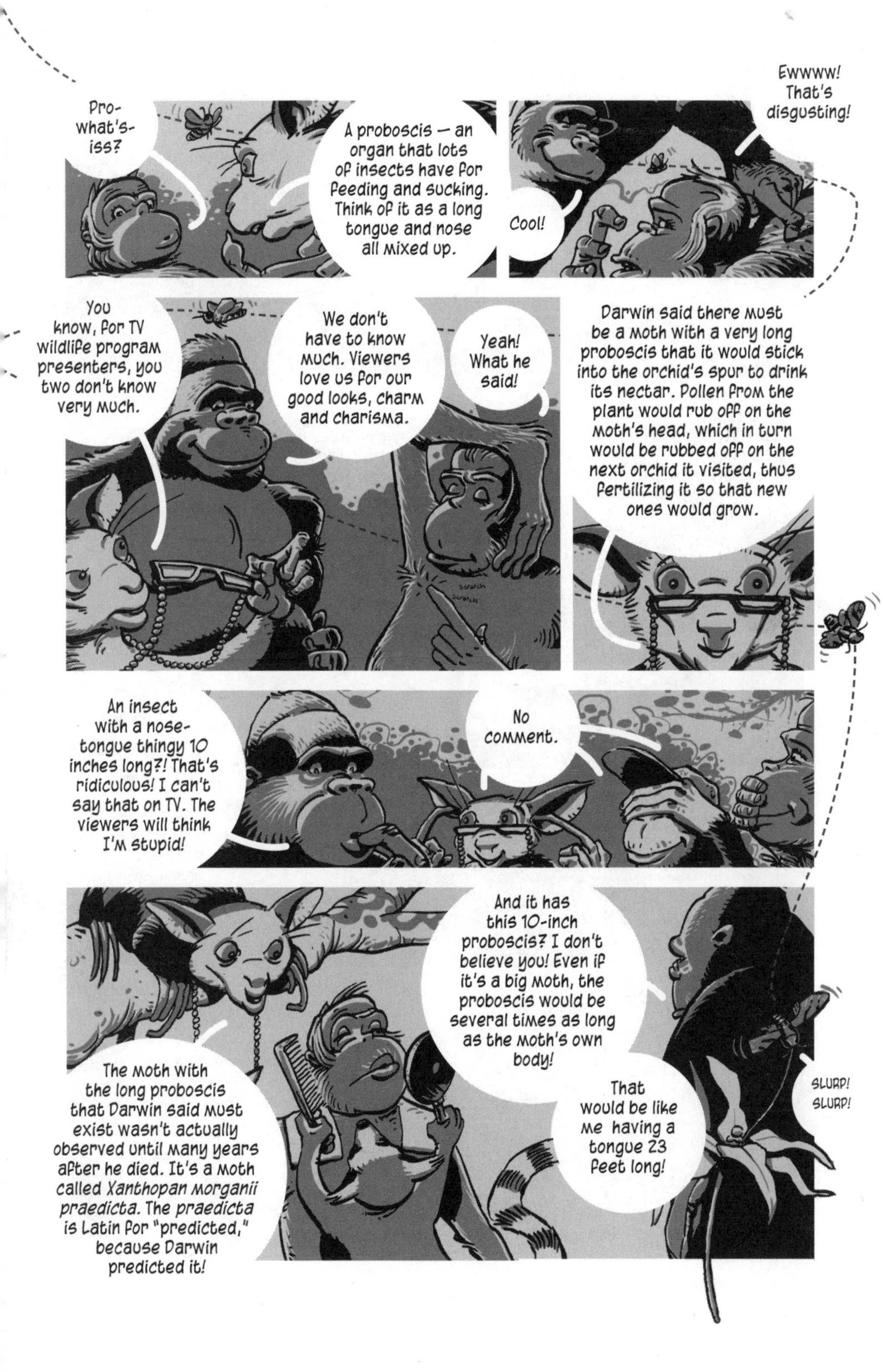
Pro-what's-iss?
A proboscis — an organ that lots of insects have for feeding and sucking. Think of it as a long tongue and nose all mixed up.
Cool!
Ewwww! That's disgusting!
You know, for TV wildlife program presenters, you two don't know very much.
We don't have to know much. Viewers love us for our good looks, charm and charisma.
Yeah! What he said!
Darwin said there must be a moth with a very long proboscis that it would stick into the orchid's spur to drink its nectar. Pollen from the plant would rub off on the moth's head, which in turn would be rubbed off on the next orchid it visited, thus fertilizing it so that new ones would grow.
An insect with a nose-tongue thingy 10 inches long?! That's ridiculous! I can't say that on TV. The viewers will think I'm stupid!
No comment.
And it has this 10-inch proboscis? I don't believe you! Even if it's a big moth, the proboscis would be several times as long as the moth's own body!
That would be like me having a tongue 23 feet long!
SLURP! SLURP!
The moth with the long proboscis that Darwin said must exist wasn't actually observed until many years after he died. It's a moth called *Xanthopan morganii praedicta*. The *praedicta* is Latin for "predicted," because Darwin predicted it!

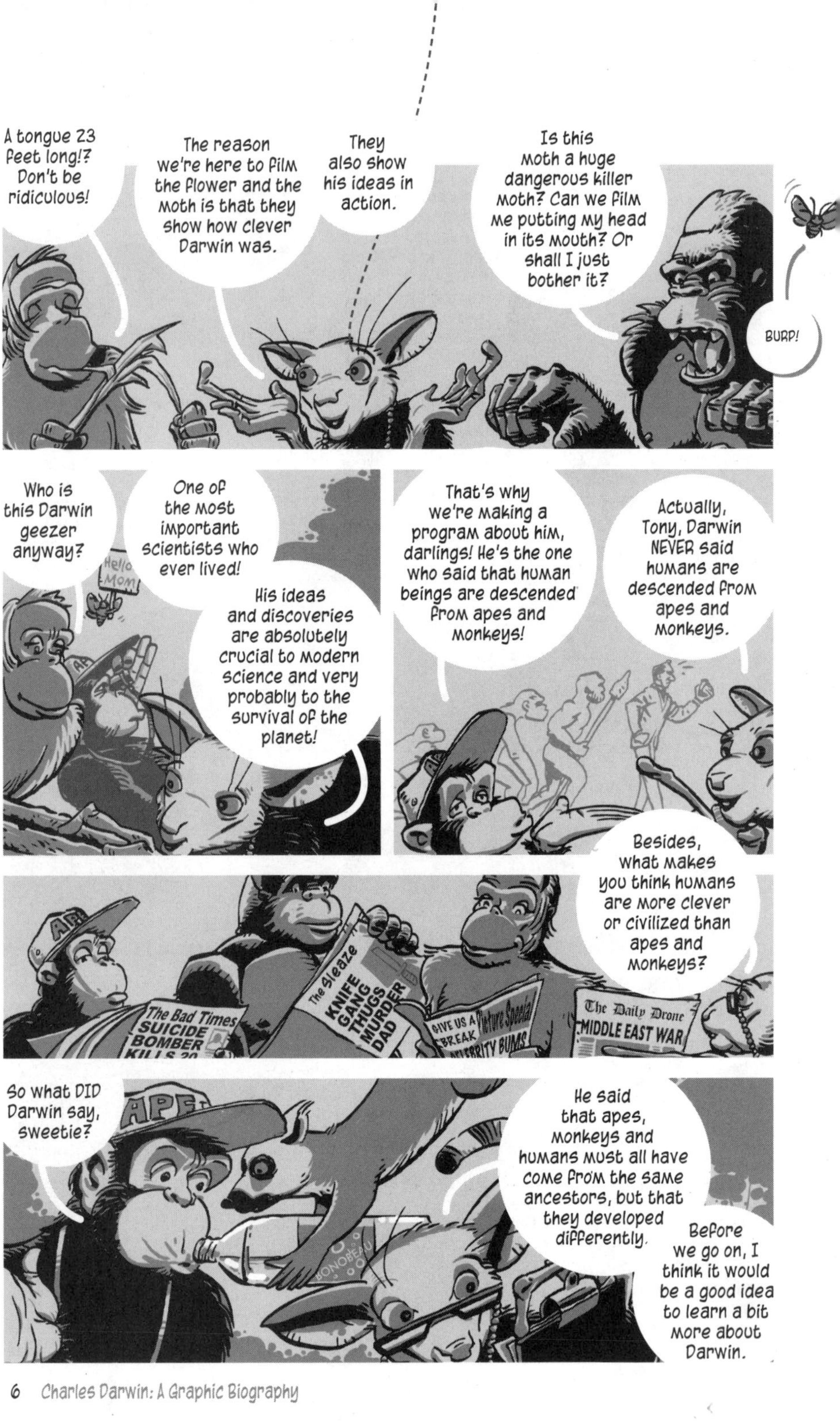
A tongue 23 feet long!? Don't be ridiculous!
The reason we're here to film the flower and the moth is that they show how clever Darwin was.
They also show his ideas in action.
Is this moth a huge dangerous killer moth? Can we film me putting my head in its mouth? Or shall I just bother it?
BURP!
Who is this Darwin geezer anyway?
Hello Mom
One of the most important scientists who ever lived!
His ideas and discoveries are absolutely crucial to modern science and very probably to the survival of the planet!
That's why we're making a program about him, darlings! He's the one who said that human beings are descended from apes and monkeys!
Actually, Tony, Darwin NEVER said humans are descended from apes and monkeys.
Besides, what makes you think humans are more clever or civilized than apes and monkeys?
The Bad Times
SUICIDE BOMBER
The Sleaze
KNIFE GANG THUGS MURDER DAD
GIVE US A BREAK
Picture Special
The Daily Drone
MIDDLE EAST WAR
So what DID Darwin say, sweetie?
APE
He said that apes, monkeys and humans must all have come from the same ancestors, but that they developed differently.
Before we go on, I think it would be a good idea to learn a bit more about Darwin.

The world around us has all sorts of wonderful plants and animals — just take a look in the park or the yard.

Everyday backyard wildlife might seem boring compared to whales and tigers and polar bears, but it's not. If you take a really good look at all the different animals, plants, birds and insects around us, you'll be amazed at it, and at how well everything is adapted to its environment.

What's also amazing is how complex this life is. Look at the intricate patterns on the leaves of the most boring-looking weed, for instance. Or admire the tiny, complicated body parts of the friendly wasps*.

* This is a joke. Wasps aren't friendly. If you bother a wasp it'll sting you.
** Yes, we know that you know that wasps can sting. But the Health & Safety people said we had to warn you anyway.
*** Also, we might get sued. Like if some kid is stung after reading this, his or her parents might try to sue us for a million dollars for the time they had to spend kissing it better.
**** That's parents kissing the sting better. Not kissing the wasp better. Obviously.
***** Don't kiss wasps. Seriously. Just don't.

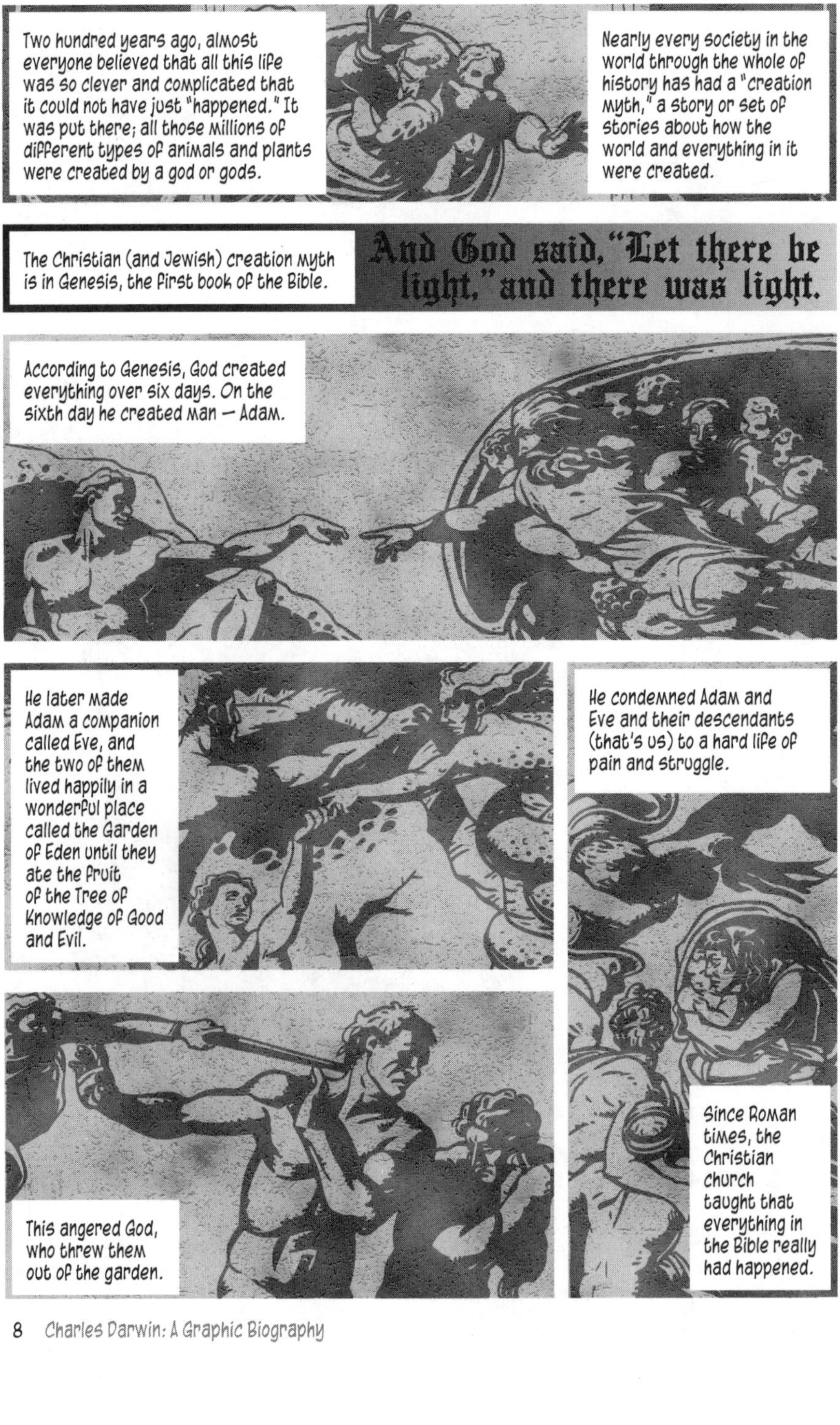
Two hundred years ago, almost everyone believed that all this life was so clever and complicated that it could not have just "happened." It was put there; all those millions of different types of animals and plants were created by a god or gods.
Nearly every society in the world through the whole of history has had a "creation myth," a story or set of stories about how the world and everything in it were created.
The Christian (and Jewish) creation myth is in Genesis, the first book of the Bible.
And God said, "Let there be light," and there was light.
According to Genesis, God created everything over six days. On the sixth day he created man — Adam.
He later made Adam a companion called Eve, and the two of them lived happily in a wonderful place called the Garden of Eden until they ate the fruit of the Tree of Knowledge of Good and Evil.
This angered God, who threw them out of the garden.
He condemned Adam and Eve and their descendants (that's us) to a hard life of pain and struggle.
Since Roman times, the Christian church taught that everything in the Bible really had happened.

But as the centuries passed, questions were raised about how true some of the Old Testament — the part of the Bible about the time before Jesus was born — really is.

For instance, the astronomers Nicolaus Copernicus (1473-1543) and Galileo Galilei (1564-1642) had shown that the Earth revolves around the sun. But the Bible says the Earth does not move, and the Catholic Church actually forced Galileo to say he was wrong.

It does move, you know.

What did you say!?

Nothing.

The church eventually had to admit that Galileo was right.

The Protestant and Catholic churches in Europe and America were equally strong in their defense of Genesis. God had created all the animals, birds, fish, insects, trees and plants of the world, and EVERYTHING had been the same ever since the day he had made them.

In Britain they even thought they knew exactly when God had created the Earth. The date had been worked out in the 1640s by Bishop James Ussher.

He began the Creation at six o'clock on the evening of Saturday October 22, 4004 BC.

Nowadays we know the Earth is much, much older — about 4.54 billion years — and most people think Ussher is laughable. To be fair, he was a brilliant scholar who made his calculation using ancient historical writings as well as the Bible. He does not deserve to be ridiculed for a mistake based on the best knowledge people had at the time.

But by the late 1700s, more and more "naturalists" — people who studied nature — were starting to question the truth of Genesis and to question the church teaching that nothing on Earth had ever changed.

Anyone who studied nature could see that landscapes and environments had changed over time — and so had the animals living in them.

What about earthquakes, for instance? These often changed the landscapes they affected. Or volcanoes?

And what about fossils? Fossils appeared to be the remains of plants and creatures that had existed thousands, or even millions of years ago. Many of these were of creatures that clearly did not exist anymore.

The church had a couple of responses to this:

Fossils are the remains of the animals which did not manage to get onto Noah's Ark during the Great Flood, which you can read about in Genesis.

God has placed fossils in the rocks for decoration!

Besides, people had been "selectively breeding" plants and animals for thousands of years to improve crops to yield more food, or to resist bad weather and disease. People bred stronger, faster horses, or cattle that produced more milk, or sheep with better wool, or pigs with more meat ...

A good example of selective breeding is the dog. Wild dogs were first domesticated by man thousands of years ago for jobs like hunting, herding animals, guarding farm animals from predators and so on. Nowadays we talk about different "breeds" of dog because that's exactly what they are — they have been bred over the years for different roles. Males and females with desirable traits, such as strength, speed, aggression or intelligence, are mated with each other to breed new generations that are stronger, faster, or more aggressive or intelligent.

Arrr ... I'm trying to breed a dog that'll herd the sheep and can fill in my tax forms.

We're not quite there yet.

And, of course, if you go to a dog show, you'll see all sorts of weird and wonderful animals — many of them have been specially bred as show dogs.

So not all plants and animals were the same as they had always been, because new ones were being made all the time through selective breeding.

And if human beings could change living things over the years, why couldn't nature do it as well?

By 1800 even a few church leaders wondered if Genesis was literally true. But even if it wasn't, few people doubted that God had designed the world and everything in it.

Anyone questioning Genesis had to deal with the "watchmaker argument."

This idea was most famously put forward by a churchman named William Paley (1743-1805), whose books were hugely popular.

Imagine you are walking through the countryside and find a watch lying on the ground.

You pick it up and examine it and see that it's made of various materials — glass, and different types of metal. You open it up and see that it contains a complicated mechanism of springs, cogs and gears.

You wouldn't think the watch had just "happened," would you?

You would know that this intricate piece of machinery has been designed and made by an intelligent being.

Well, it's the same with animals. Look at how wonderfully complicated the internal organs of a human being or animal are. Look at how well all the plants and animals fit into their environments.

All life, and the whole universe — the sun, moon and stars — are all so complex and work so perfectly that they MUST have been made by a designer.

And that designer is, of course, God.

When Charles Darwin was born in 1809, most people lived in small towns or villages. Ideas, information and news did not spread quickly. Travel was expensive and difficult as there were no decent roads, and a journey of even 10 miles was a big adventure.

This started to change with the industrial revolution.

"Industrial revolution" is the term for a number of changes in farming, manufacturing and transportation in the 1700s and 1800s that had a huge effect on the way people lived. Improvements in mining and metallurgy (the science of metals) and the development of steam engines meant that simple, repetitive work that had once been done by human hands was now done by machines. Factories were built to make everything from cloth to pottery, to buttons and belt buckles cheaply and in large quantities.

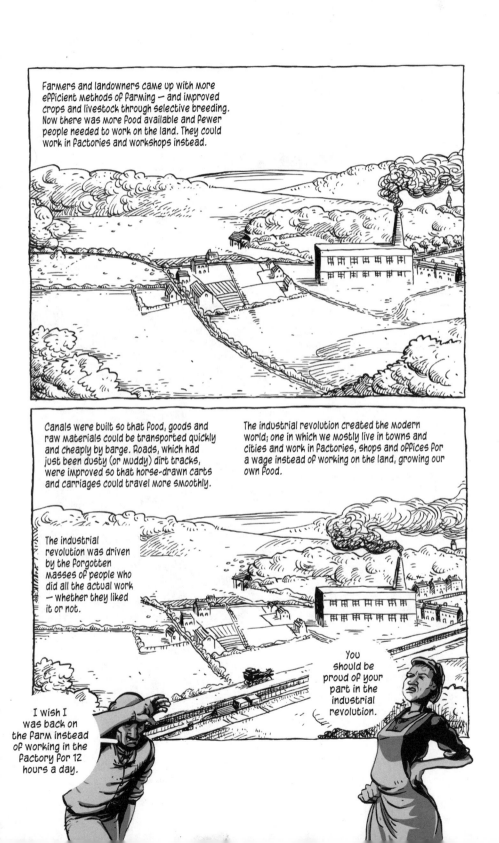

Farmers and landowners came up with more efficient methods of farming – and improved crops and livestock through selective breeding. Now there was more food available and fewer people needed to work on the land. They could work in factories and workshops instead.

Canals were built so that food, goods and raw materials could be transported quickly and cheaply by barge. Roads, which had just been dusty (or muddy) dirt tracks, were improved so that horse-drawn carts and carriages could travel more smoothly.

The industrial revolution created the modern world; one in which we mostly live in towns and cities and work in factories, shops and offices for a wage instead of working on the land, growing our own food.

The industrial revolution was driven by the forgotten masses of people who did all the actual work – whether they liked it or not.

I wish I was back on the farm instead of working in the factory for 12 hours a day.

You should be proud of your part in the industrial revolution.

The industrial revolution was based on knowledge — on advances in science, technology and understanding of the natural world.

Developments in science, engineering and invention came from careful observation and measurement. One particular man is a very good example of the way in which the industrial revolution, business and the rise of science come together — Erasmus Darwin.

Erasmus Darwin (1731-1802) was born in Nottinghamshire, England, educated at Chesterfield Grammar School and Cambridge University. He went on to study at Edinburgh Medical School and set himself up as a doctor in Lichfield in Staffordshire. He was very successful.

Erasmus Darwin was also a naturalist, philosopher, inventor and poet. He married twice and had lots of children.

Erasmus Darwin was fascinated by new knowledge and was one of the founders of the famous Lunar Society. This was a group of scientists, inventors, businessmen and thinkers who met every month during the full moon (so that they could see their way home again at night — there was no street lighting in those days).

At one time or another, the "lunatics," as they jokingly called themselves, included many of the most important figures in the industrial revolution.

There was the Birmingham industrialist Matthew Boulton,

and his business partner the engineer James Watt (inventor of an improved steam engine),

the scientist and political thinker Joseph Priestley (who discovered oxygen),

the engineer John Smeaton,

the painter Joseph Wright and many others.

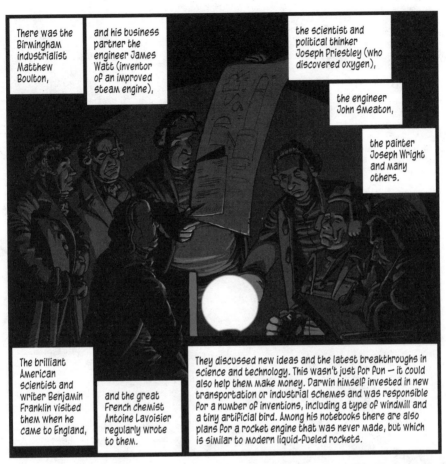

The brilliant American scientist and writer Benjamin Franklin visited them when he came to England,

and the great French chemist Antoine Lavoisier regularly wrote to them.

They discussed new ideas and the latest breakthroughs in science and technology. This wasn't just for fun — it could also help them make money. Darwin himself invested in new transportation or industrial schemes and was responsible for a number of inventions, including a type of windmill and a tiny artificial bird. Among his notebooks there are also plans for a rocket engine that was never made, but which is similar to modern liquid-fueled rockets.

Erasmus Darwin also wrote books and poems about his studies of nature. In his book *Zoönomia* he put forward a theory of evolution, that is, he said that plants and animals do change and develop over time. He suggested that all life on Earth came from a single original organism or cause. His long poem "The Temple of Nature" expanded the idea:

First forms minute, unseen by spheric glass,
Move on the mud, or pierce the watery mass;
These, as successive generations bloom,
New powers acquire, and larger limbs assume;
Whence countless groups of vegetation spring,
And breathing realms of fin, and feet, and wing.

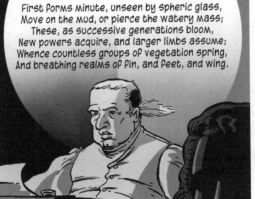

So Erasmus Darwin said that life on Earth hadn't been put there as fully formed plants and animals by God. He was saying that plants and animals had evolved over the centuries, having started out as microscopic life-forms.

Stop, stop! I'm confused. I thought a bearded fellow called Charles Darwin had the theory of evolution, not a fat fellow called Erasmus Darwin!

You're right. We're only mentioning Erasmus Darwin to show that before Charles Darwin was born people were already wondering about how life on Earth had developed.

Erasmus Darwin was very famous in his time.

There was also a Frenchman named Jean-Baptiste Pierre Antoine de Monet, Chevalier de Lamarck who said that all animals are influenced by their environment.

So what's so important about Charles Darwin if other people had theories of evolution before him?

Because Charles Darwin worked out *how* evolution happens.

Lamarck said that animals were evolving and getting better and better all the time.

Helen, sweetie, are Erasmus and Charles Darwin related, by any chance?

Yes. Can we get back to the story now?

One of Erasmus Darwin's best friends was Josiah Wedgwood, another member of the Lunar Society. Wedgwood was a hugely important figure in the industrial revolution because he led the way in using factory methods to produce pottery.

Everyone needs plates and cups and teapots and his business was very successful.

In 1796 Erasmus's son Robert married Josiah Wedgwood's daughter Susannah.

Robert Darwin was, like his father, a doctor. He set up a successful practice and in 1800 he and Susannah moved to The Mount, the house they had had built for themselves at Shrewsbury, in the West Midlands of England.

Robert and Susannah Darwin had four daughters and two sons. The second son, Charles Robert Darwin, was born at The Mount on February 12, 1809.

WAAAAAAAAAAAAAAAA

Here we see the young human having just hatched out.

Is it dangerous? Does it have a poisonous bite? I can pick it up and show the viewers how fearless I am.

The really fearless thing to do would be to change its diaper.

Charles Darwin had a happy childhood.

He was fond of mischief.

One of his earliest memories was trying to break the window of a room he'd been locked in as a punishment.

He later said:

As a little boy I was much given to inventing deliberate falsehoods, and this was always done for the sake of causing excitement.

For instance, I once gathered much valuable fruit from my father's trees and hid it in the shrubbery, and then ran in breathless haste to spread the news that I had discovered a hoard of stolen fruit.

His mother died when he was eight years old. We don't know what effect this had on him, because in later life he said that he didn't remember much about her.

His three older sisters — Marianne, Caroline and Susan — took over running the home, and looking after Charles, his older brother Erasmus (always known in the family as Eras), youngest sister Emily Catherine, and of course their father.

Charles and Eras went to school in Shrewsbury. When Charles was nine he joined his older brother at Shrewsbury Grammar School, run by the Reverend Samuel Butler.

Even though he was five years older than Charles, Eras was his best friend. During the school vacations, they even set up a laboratory at home where they did their own chemistry experiments. Charles's schoolmates knew all about his love of chemistry. They nicknamed him "Gas."

Schools then were very different from now. Schools had to be paid for (though there were a few free places for bright boys paid for by charities or wealthy people) and many children had no education at all. Girls in rich families rarely went to school, but were educated at home. Most children from working families had little or no education, and many Britons in the early 1800s could not read and write.

Dr. Butler's school was keen on the "classics" — Greek and Latin, and the history, myths and literature of ancient Greece and Rome. Students did study math, and some geography, but subjects like science were non-existent.

As far as everyone was concerned, Charles and Eras's chemistry lab was not educational or useful, but an expensive and time-wasting hobby.

Brevis ipsa vita est sed malis fit longior.

Publilius S.

HOMER

Nowadays, we have even more educational ways of wasting time.

Young gentlemen do not need to know about smells and explosions. They need an understanding of ancient civilizations to help them become the future leaders of the British Empire.

Or the future leaders of Shrewsbury, anyway.

Charles Darwin did not do well at school. The classics bored him and he absolutely hated math. He preferred his chemistry, or going for long walks, and collecting rocks, coins and birds' eggs.

As a teenager, he also loved shooting. During the season, he would go with family and friends and blast partridge and other birds out of the sky on the estates of nearby landowners. It was what rich country gentlemen did for fun in those days.

Apparently this is a very enjoyable sport, though I can't say I'm all that crazy about it.

When Charles was 16, his father decided he had had enough schooling. It was time to study for a career.

Eras was studying to become a doctor like his father, and Robert decided that Charles should do the same. Charles Darwin spent the summer of 1825 learning the basics of medicine as an assistant to his father. He even had his own patients to look after.

Imagine being treated by a 16-year-old doctor!

Robert Darwin was a big man in the neighborhood. He was a successful and popular doctor and owned a lot of property, which he rented out. He also invested his money wisely on the stock market.

He was six feet two inches tall and got fatter as he got older. He stopped weighing himself after he reached 336 pounds — and put on a lot more weight after that.

He had special stone steps made for him to enter his carriage, and when he went out visiting his patients, he had to have his coachman (who was also rather large) go into the house first to check that the floorboards were strong enough to take his weight!

Darwin remembered his father as a kindly, clever man who understood his patients well and was an excellent judge of other people.

But he had a very short temper, and he often despaired that his son would never do anything useful with his life.

You care for nothing but shooting, dogs, and rat-catching, and you will be a disgrace to yourself and all your family!

At the end of summer, it was time for some proper medical training, and Charles was sent off to study in Edinburgh.

Eras was already there completing his own medical studies. The brothers lived together at 11 Lothian Street, close to the university.

Darwin's medical training went no better than his classical studies at school. He found the lectures boring.

He also hated the sight of blood. Operations in those days were very crude; most surgery simply involved cutting off injured or diseased arms or legs to prevent the spread of infection and save the patient's life. It was done without any anesthetic; many died from the pain and shock.

At medical schools, operations were carried out in front of an audience of students — that's why we still call it an operating "theater."

He had to watch an operation being carried out on a child who was terrified and in terrible pain. It disturbed him so much that he ran out.

Gruesome Footnote: The best way for medical students — and physicians and surgeons doing medical research — to find out how the human body worked was to cut one open. At this time, the law allowed for the bodies of criminals who had been executed (usually by hanging) to be handed over to doctors and surgeons for dissection. But by now there were fewer executions and more students, so there were never enough corpses.

Some people stole bodies of innocent people from graves, which they sold to medical schools for money.

In Edinburgh at this time, two men found an even easier way to make cash than grave robbing. William Burke and William Hare sold the bodies of 17 people to Edinburgh Medical School, most of them to Dr. Robert Knox. What Knox didn't know was that Burke and Hare had actually murdered most of them. They were eventually found out; Hare confessed and gave evidence against Burke in return for his freedom. Burke was hanged in January 1829.

Of course, his body was dissected for the benefit of Edinburgh's medical students.

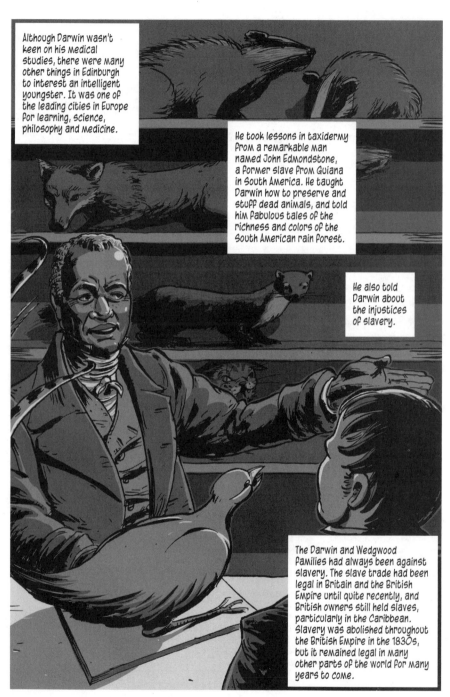

Although Darwin wasn't keen on his medical studies, there were many other things in Edinburgh to interest an intelligent youngster. It was one of the leading cities in Europe for learning, science, philosophy and medicine.

He took lessons in taxidermy from a remarkable man named John Edmondstone, a former slave from Guiana in South America. He taught Darwin how to preserve and stuff dead animals, and told him fabulous tales of the richness and colors of the South American rain forest.

He also told Darwin about the injustices of slavery.

The Darwin and Wedgwood families had always been against slavery. The slave trade had been legal in Britain and the British Empire until quite recently, and British owners still held slaves, particularly in the Caribbean. Slavery was abolished throughout the British Empire in the 1830s, but it remained legal in many other parts of the world for many years to come.

By his second year at Edinburgh, Darwin was far more interested in naturalism than medicine. His brother had left for London to study, and he now spent a lot of time in the university museum looking at the plants and animals. He also joined a club called the Plinian Society, which held scientific talks and discussions.

He became friendly with an older scientist named Robert Grant. Grant was a "freethinker," one of a small number of people who said that not everything in the Bible was necessarily true, and that the only way to understand the world was by scientific observation. Grant was also a follower of Lamarck, the French naturalist who had said that animals were evolving all the time.

Grant was a doctor, but spent most of his time studying simple sea creatures like sponges and polyps, because he believed that all life on Earth had evolved from these very basic life-forms. Darwin spent a lot of time with Grant and would join him on the seashore on his expeditions looking for specimens.

Meanwhile, though, his medical studies were being neglected. In the spring of 1827, he dropped out for good. He would never, he decided, become a doctor.

For most young men in this situation, this would have been a disaster. He had no career, no real idea of what he wanted to do with his life, and no way of earning a living.

But Charles Darwin was from a rich family. He secretly felt that he didn't have to work too hard at anything because his father would look after him anyway.

After dropping out of Edinburgh, he visited London for the first time. Then he joined his uncle, Josiah Wedgwood II on a trip to Paris.

He also started to notice Fanny Owen, a friend of one of his sisters. Fanny was the daughter of a wealthy landowner who lived near the Darwin home in Shropshire. They went out riding together, they played billiards, they shot birds ...

Ahh, how very romantic!

Robert Darwin was not pleased.

I am not pleased.

I will not see my son turning into an idle gentleman.

I have decided you shall become a clergyman.

What? Me? A vicar?

Why not? It is the ideal career for a young man who does not know what to do with himself. As the parson of a country parish you shall be respectable and useful ...

And there will be ample time for your other interests — catching beetles and shooting birds and whatever else.

It is a very practical suggestion, father.

Yes, it is. Your older brother is at Cambridge. That is where you shall go too. The entrance examinations are in December. I suggest you start studying for them now.

Do not fail me this time.

He passed the entrance exam (just!) and arrived at Christ's College in early 1828 to study for a career as a clergyman.

Cambridge was a place with a lot of temptations — and Darwin was tempted.

During the three years which I spent at Cambridge my time was wasted, as far as the academical studies were concerned, as completely as at Edinburgh and at school.

So what was it that Darwin took up instead? Drinking? Gambling? Eating? Chasing after the young ladies of the town? (There were no female students.) What sort of riotous living did he get into?

He collected beetles.

At this time, "beetling" was a huge craze among people with the time and money to do it. Enthusiasts would travel a long way to hunt for rare or unusual species.

Darwin was swept away by the craze. He often went out beetling with his cousin, William Darwin Fox, who was also a student at Cambridge.

One day he was out collecting, and had two rare beetles, one in each hand. Suddenly he saw a third one on a dead tree. It was too good to lose, but he didn't have a free hand ... So he put the beetle from his right hand into his mouth. Unfortunately, it turned out to be a bombardier beetle.

Worldwide, there are hundreds of different species of bombardier beetle, but they all have the same way of defending themselves. They have two tubes in their abdomen, which squirt two separate chemicals — hydrogen peroxide and hydroquinone. When mixed together, along with tiny amounts of enzymes (molecules which speed up chemical reactions), they turn into a hot, stinking mixture of liquid and gas.

And that's what happened in Darwin's mouth that day. He was stunned for a while and lost all three of his precious beetles.

His cousin Fox also introduced him to one of the most important influences on his life, the Reverend John Stevens Henslow.

Henslow was 32 but already professor of botany at Cambridge. He was regarded as one of the country's leading scientists, and Darwin started going to Henslow's lectures.

That summer, he went to Wales. Being a wealthy young gentleman, he took a math tutor with him so that he could try and come to grips with algebra, which he found very difficult. Then he took a vacation at Barmouth with his friends and returned home, spending a lot of time with Fanny Owen. He even took her beetle hunting, though we don't know how interesting she found it.

When he returned to Cambridge, he neglected his studies and spent his time collecting beetles, studying nature and having fun. He drank, dined and gambled with friends. They were fond of a card game they called "Van John" — an English corruption of "vingt-et-un," the French for 21 — we call it blackjack.

Even Darwin's high living had a scientific flavor to it. He and some friends had started the Glutton Club and every week they met for dinner. The idea behind the Glutton Club was not to eat too much, but to eat things which people didn't normally eat. They would get a chef to cook them some exotic animal, and then sit down and dive in.

It all came to a nasty end after they ate an elderly brown owl. They decided to stick to a more normal menu after that.

Very wise.

Henslow recognized that Darwin was a brilliant student, even if he didn't work very hard. Darwin went to all of Henslow's botany lectures and the two of them often went for long walks or plant-collecting expeditions together.

Henslow also gave him private lessons to help him through his final exams. In the months before the exams, he worked very hard.

To Darwin, the future seemed clear. He would become a clergyman in the countryside and devote his spare time to studying nature — just like his great hero Henslow.

He passed, coming in 10th out of 178 students.

He wasn't in a hurry to start work for the church just yet. For fun, he was reading a lot of books about wildlife and nature, including the massive book that the German explorer and naturalist Alexander von Humboldt had written about his discoveries in South America.

He dreamed of visiting tropical rain forests. Henslow suggested that he should go and explore the tropics for a while before starting his church career. Darwin thought this was a splendid idea, and decided that he should explore Tenerife in the Canary Islands.

(Tenerife is a popular vacation destination nowadays, but in 1831, when overseas travel could only be done by slow-moving sailing ships, it was a faraway place and nobody knew much about its geology, plant or animal life.)

Darwin's father said he would pay for the trip — probably. He was relieved that his son had passed his exams well and was now on the way to a proper career and adult responsibility.

Darwin's friend Marmaduke Ramsay, a tutor at Jesus College, would go with him. Meanwhile, Henslow recommended that Darwin learn more about geology before he went, and introduced him to Adam Sedgwick, Cambridge's professor of geology.

In August, Darwin and Sedgwick spent a week together in North Wales, looking at different types of rock, and at the fossils and bones of extinct animals.

Darwin became fascinated by the questions of how the Earth had been formed.

All our knowledge about the structure of the Earth is very much like what an old hen would know of the hundred-acre field in a corner of which she is scratching.

After his week with Sedgwick, he joined some friends in Barmouth for two weeks of drinking, eating and field sport. Then came terrible news: Marmaduke Ramsay had died.

Darwin headed home for Shrewsbury, feeling very depressed. He was saddened by the loss of his friend, but also devastated by the end of their plans to travel to Tenerife together. In the meantime, his romance with Fanny Owen had ended as well, though we still don't really know why.

But when he got home, he found a letter from Henslow waiting for him. It would not just change Darwin's life, it would change the course of history.

Charles Darwin Esq.
The Mount
Shrewsbury
Shropshire

CAMBRIDGE

Cambridge, 24 Aug 1831

My dear Darwin,

... you will eagerly catch at the offer which is likely to be made you of a trip to Terra del Fuego & home by the East Indies - I have been asked to recommend a naturalist as companion to Capt FitzRoy employed by Government to survey the S. extremity of America -

Thanks to the industrial revolution, Britain in 1831 was the most wealthy and powerful nation on Earth. Goods, food, drink and raw materials were carried to and from British ports in sailing ships. This huge trade was protected by the Royal Navy.

Now, many new countries in South America, which had once been part of the empires of Spain and Portugal, had freed themselves from their European masters.

... I consider you to be the best qualified person I know of ... I state this not on the supposition of yr. being a finished Naturalist, but as amply qualified for collecting, observing, & noting any thing worthy to be noted in Natural History.

British businesses wanted to trade with these countries. If British merchants were going there, the Navy had to be there, too. Britain's merchant ships and warships would need maps of the coastline, with details of tides, beaches, rivers, currents and the depth of water in every spot.

Because much of South America had never been properly explored, the Navy sent ships to survey the coast and produce hydrographic charts — maps for use by shipping.

Darwin was being offered a trip around the world on one of these survey ships.

Capt. F. wants a man (I understand) more as a companion than a mere collector & would not take any one however good a Naturalist who was not recommended to him likewise as a gentleman.

In 1831, people traveled at the speed of horses, sailing ships or their own feet (although Britain was now building the world's first railways). The world was a huge place, and this was the chance of a lifetime.

A trip around the world even nowadays is a big adventure, but in 1831 it was almost unimaginable. Very few people had ever circumnavigated — traveled all the way around — the globe. Of those who had, almost all were professional sailors, not landlubbers like Darwin.

The Voyage is to last 2 yrs. & if you take plenty of Books with you, any thing you please may be done - You will have ample opportunities at command - In short I suppose there never was a finer chance for a man of zeal & spirit. Capt F. is a young man.

Think of it in modern terms as being given the chance to travel into space.

Don't put on any modest doubts or fears about your disqualifications for I assure you I think you are the very man they are in search of ...

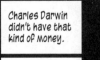

J. S. Henslow

Darwin was thrilled. But there were problems; he wouldn't be able to start his church career yet. He would also have to pay the Navy for his accommodation and food, buy all his own clothes and equipment and pay any bills he ran up on the journey.

Charles Darwin didn't have that kind of money.

But he knew a man who did.

I cannot give this jaunt my blessing. It will spoil your chances of making a good career in the church.

Besides, sailors are coarse, hard-living men who drink too much. Years spent in their company will corrupt you.

Darwin felt crushed. He went off to see his uncle Josiah Wedgwood II at his estates in Staffordshire for a bit of hunting.

Take it out on us, why don't you?

What Darwin didn't know was that his father had written to Josiah asking his advice on the matter.

"Uncle Jos" thought Charles should go. He wrote back saying the experience would do Charles a lot of good. If he had seen a lot of the world, he would be much better qualified to be a vicar.

But of course you and Charles must decide ...

Robert Darwin respected Uncle Jos's opinions. He gave the voyage his blessing and would pay all the expenses.

He's leaving the country! Excellent!!

Darwin excitedly went to London to meet the leader of the expedition, Commander Robert FitzRoy.

FitzRoy was only four years older than Darwin, but had led a very different life. He had joined the Navy at the age of 12, and had already spent many years at sea. He came from a very wealthy aristocratic family, with friends and family members at the highest levels of government and the Navy.

FitzRoy was utterly dedicated to his work and was a devout Christian. He was serious, strict and had a terrible temper. But the men who sailed with him respected him as an excellent sailor, navigator and leader.

From 1826 to 1830 FitzRoy had served on HMS Beagle, a ship surveying the coast of Patagonia (now part of Argentina) and Tierra del Fuego at the southernmost tip of South America.

Now Beagle was going to South America again to complete the work.

FitzRoy wanted a companion because he had a stressful and lonely job. He and his men would be at sea for years, jammed together in very cramped conditions. FitzRoy could not become too friendly with other crewmen because that would undermine his authority. But he knew he had to have someone he could talk to as an equal.

Because he was interested in science and nature himself, and because naturalists often went on Navy expeditions, FitzRoy had asked around for a gentleman-naturalist as a companion; Henslow had heard about it and recommended Darwin.

Meeting FitzRoy for the first time, Darwin was overawed. They went around London together, buying the clothes, supplies and scientific equipment Darwin would need on the voyage.

His enthusiasm for the journey started to wane when he accompanied FitzRoy to Plymouth and first saw the Beagle.

Beagle was tiny; 90 feet long and 24 feet 6 inches wide — smaller than a full-grown blue whale. This little ship had to accommodate 74 people.

To the Navy, she was a 10-gun Cherokee-class brig. To the sailors, she was a "coffin brig." Ships of Beagle's type were difficult to handle in rough weather and had a nasty habit of capsizing.

But Commander FitzRoy wasn't going to let that happen. He spent huge amounts of his own money making improvements so that Beagle would handle better.

FitzRoy was a keen amateur scientist, and in later life pioneered Britain's first weather-forecasting system. He saved the lives of thousands of sailors and fishermen by giving advance warnings of storms.

Because Beagle's mission was to produce the most accurate maps possible, FitzRoy left nothing to chance. He replaced her 10 iron cannon with 6 brass ones, partly to make more room, but also because brass is not magnetic and would not interfere with the ship's compasses and chronometers.*

HMS Beagle

* Chronometer — an extremely accurate clock enabling ships to fix their precise longitude. The Royal Navy's secret weapon in the late 1700s and early 1800s because it meant British ships could navigate far better than rival nations' warships. FitzRoy had 22 of them on Beagle.

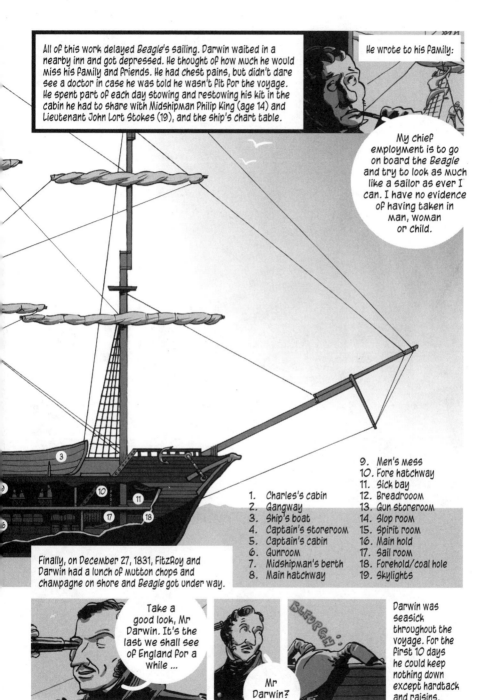

All of this work delayed *Beagle's* sailing. Darwin waited in a nearby inn and got depressed. He thought of how much he would miss his family and friends. He had chest pains, but didn't dare see a doctor in case he was told he wasn't fit for the voyage. He spent part of each day stowing and restowing his kit in the cabin he had to share with Midshipman Philip King (age 14) and Lieutenant John Lort Stokes (19), and the ship's chart table.

He wrote to his family:

My chief employment is to go on board the *Beagle* and try to look as much like a sailor as ever I can. I have no evidence of having taken in man, woman or child.

1. Charles's cabin
2. Gangway
3. Ship's boat
4. Captain's storeroom
5. Captain's cabin
6. Gunroom
7. Midshipman's berth
8. Main hatchway
9. Men's mess
10. Fore hatchway
11. Sick bay
12. Breadrooom
13. Gun storeroom
14. Slop room
15. Spirit room
16. Main hold
17. Sail room
18. Forehold/coal hole
19. Skylights

Finally, on December 27, 1831, FitzRoy and Darwin had a lunch of mutton chops and champagne on shore and *Beagle* got under way.

Take a good look, Mr Darwin. It's the last we shall see of England for a while ...

BLEURGH!

Mr Darwin?

Darwin was seasick throughout the voyage. For the first 10 days he could keep nothing down except hardtack and raisins.

On January 16, 1832, they landed in the Cape Verde Islands.

Here I first saw the glory of tropical vegetation.

Tamarinds, Bananas & Palms were flourishing at my feet. — I expected a good deal, for I had read Humboldt's descriptions & I was afraid of disappointments: how utterly vain such fear is, none can tell but those who have experienced what I today have.

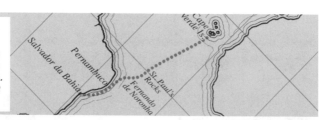

The next stop was Salvador da Bahia in Brazil, where Darwin first had the chance to explore a real tropical rain forest. He was bowled over by the colors and sheer chaos.

At Bahia he also had his first real-life encounter with slaves.

Slavery was legal in Brazil. European settlers had forced the Amazon peoples to work for them and then imported slaves from Africa. Brazil did not abolish slavery until 1888. It was also legal in the United States and would remain so until the end of the American Civil War in 1865.

Darwin was shocked. Both the Darwin and Wedgwood sides of his family had campaigned against slavery in the British Empire.

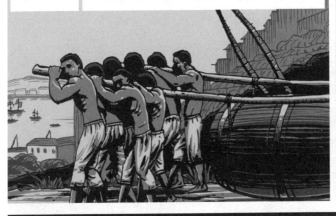

FitzRoy disliked slavery, but said that if the slaves of Brazil were freed, they would end up in starvation and poverty. Slave owners, he said, treated them well because they were valuable property.

I once heard a slave owner ask his slaves if they wanted to be free. They said they did not. Should we not respect the wishes of the slaves?

They would have been terrified of being punished by their owner. What is a slave's answer worth in his master's presence?

It makes my blood boil to think that we Englishmen and our American descendants, with their boastful cry of "liberty," have been — and are — so guilty.

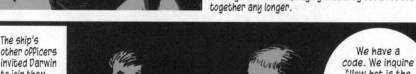

FitzRoy stormed out, saying that they could not live together any longer.

The ship's other officers invited Darwin to join them.

We have a code. We inquire "How hot is the coffee today?" when we want to know how bad the captain's temper is.

FitzRoy apologized a few hours later and they made up, but the two were never quite as friendly again.

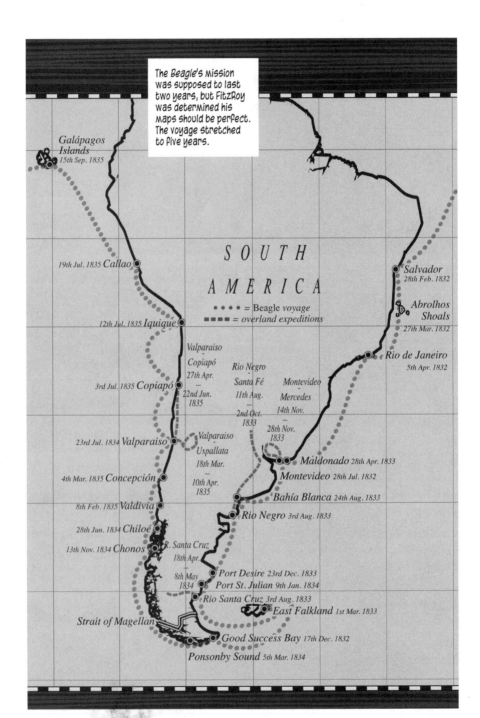

The Beagle's mission was supposed to last two years, but FitzRoy was determined his maps should be perfect. The voyage stretched to five years.

Galápagos Islands 15th Sep. 1835

S O U T H

A M E R I C A

19th Jul. 1835 Callao

• • • • = Beagle voyage
■ ■ ■ ■ = overland expeditions

Salvador 28th Feb. 1832

Abrolhos Shoals 27th Mar. 1832

12th Jul. 1835 Iquique

Valparaiso
Copiapó
27th Apr.
–
22nd Jun.
1835

Rio Negro
Santa Fé
11th Aug.
–
2nd Oct.
1833

Montevideo
Mercedes
14th Nov.

Rio de Janeiro 5th Apr. 1832

3rd Jul. 1835 Copiapó

23rd Jul. 1834 Valparaiso

Valparaiso
Uspallata
18th Mar.
–
10th Apr.
1835

28th Nov. 1833

Maldonado 28th Apr. 1833

4th Mar. 1835 Concepción

Montevideo 28th Jul. 1832

8th Feb. 1835 Valdivia

Bahía Blanca 24th Aug. 1833

Rio Negro 3rd Aug. 1833

28th Jun. 1834 Chiloé

13th Nov. 1834 Chonos

R. Santa Cruz
18th Apr.

8th May
1834

Port Desire 23rd Dec. 1833
Port St. Julian 9th Jan. 1834
Rio Santa Cruz 3rd Aug. 1833

East Falkland 1st Mar. 1833

Strait of Magellan

Good Success Bay 17th Dec. 1832

Ponsonby Sound 5th Mar. 1834

Darwin spent most of this time on land. *Beagle* was not at sea all the time, and when she was, he often traveled overland, arranging to meet her later. Sometimes he traveled with local guides, and sometimes with others from the *Beagle*.

Most of these five years were spent around the coast of South America and Darwin explored in the countries that are nowadays Brazil, Uruguay, Argentina, Chile and Peru.

geniculatus

He collected insects and animals. The animals were usually killed, skinned and stuffed or preserved in jars. These were sent back to Henslow in England. Many of these had never been seen in Britain before.

Didelphis Crassicaudata
Maldonado, Uruguay

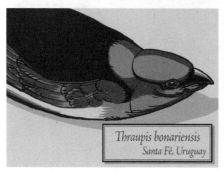

Thraupis bonariensis
Santa Fé, Uruguay

Polytrich dendroides

S. part of Tierra del Fuego, 1833

C. Darwin

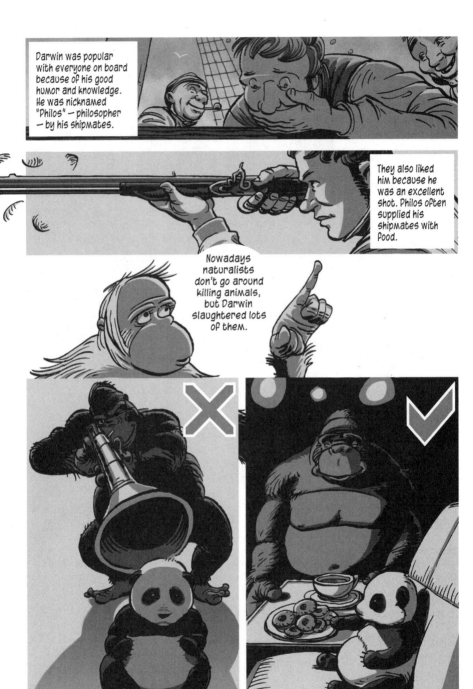

Darwin was popular with everyone on board because of his good humor and knowledge. He was nicknamed "Philos" — philosopher — by his shipmates.

They also liked him because he was an excellent shot. Philos often supplied his shipmates with food.

Nowadays naturalists don't go around killing animals, but Darwin slaughtered lots of them.

Sometimes he killed animals as specimens because they couldn't be sent back to England alive. At other times, he shot them (or killed them with a blow to the head from his geological hammer) for food. Nobody was squeamish about this; men who'd been at sea for weeks on end living on a diet of salt pork, hardtack and peas were happy with fresh meat. Of any kind.

On his travels, Darwin ate rhea, puma, armadillo, giant iguana and many other creatures. Most of South America was inhabited by few people and plenty of animals. Nobody worried about endangered species back then.

Perhaps they should have!

On one occasion, he heard the gauchos (cowboys) of northern Patagonia talking about a very rare rhea and he desperately wanted to get hold of a specimen.

One evening, he was sitting down to dinner with his shipmates when he realized that that was what they were eating.

He managed to rescue some of the bird's remains from the ship's cook to send back to Henslow.

Darwin was just as interested in geology as he was in animals. His study of rocks and fossils would be essential to his theory of evolution.

In South America he unearthed several fossils as well as non-fossilized remains of extinct animals.

One of the things he noticed was that the remains of these long-dead animals often resembled living ones. He paid a few pennies for instance, for a massive skull the size of a hippo's. It turned out later to be the head of a giant type of capybara that was long extinct.

On another occasion he found the remains of long-extinct giant armadillos the size of horses.

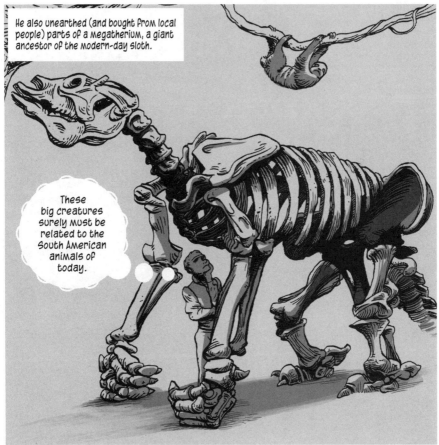

He also unearthed (and bought from local people) parts of a megatherium, a giant ancestor of the modern-day sloth.

These big creatures surely must be related to the South American animals of today.

The rocks and land itself intrigued him, too. In several places, he observed seashells on hills and in mountains.

This meant that the land had once been beneath the sea.

He journeyed, with guides and his baggage carried on mules, high up into the Andes mountains, where he again found the remains of marine life and, on one occasion, part of a fossilized forest.

So the Earth was constantly changing. Over millions of years, earthquakes and volcanic explosions and eruptions were moving seabeds into mountains, or shifting a coastline 700 miles inland.

The awesome power of nature was far easier to see on Beagle's voyage than in quiet England. The whole crew watched volcanoes spewing smoke and lava near the island of Chiloé.

In Chile, they witnessed an earthquake that completely destroyed the town of Concepción.

An earthquake like this at once destroys the oldest associations; everything that is solid moves beneath our feet like a crust over a fluid.

After the earthquake he also saw mussel beds above sea level. The earthquake had made the land rise up from the sea. This was how, eventually, you got seashells 7,000 feet up in the Andes.

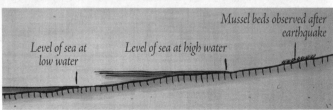

Mussel beds observed after earthquake

Level of sea at low water

Level of sea at high water

On the previous *Beagle* expedition, FitzRoy had taken four native Yaghan people from Tierra del Fuego to England. The idea was to teach the Fuegians English, convert them to Christianity and "civilize" them, and then return them home again where they could teach their fellow Fuegians about God and civilized living.

In England, one of them died, but the other three — two young men and a girl known to the sailors as Jemmy Button, York Minster and Fuegia Basket — were now being taken home. With them was also a young Christian missionary, the Reverend Richard Matthews.

In January 1833, they found a suitable place and landed the Fuegians and the reverend. The ship's crew built them huts and dug vegetable gardens as a little outpost of Christian Britain from where Matthews and the three Fuegians would convert the locals, who turned out in large numbers to see what was going on.

Beagle left Matthews there to start his missionary work and returned some days later to see how he was doing. He had been robbed of everything by the locals and rejoined the *Beagle*. Jemmy Button, York Minster and Fuegia Basket stayed with their people.

In the autumn of 1835, *Beagle* visited the Galápagos Islands for just over a month.

 Galápagos Islands

Darwin was eager to explore. There were giant tortoises that the sailors rode for amusement. He looked at giant iguanas and bothered one by grabbing it by its tail.

These islands appear paradises for the whole family of reptiles.

They were until you came along.

Can I have a turn?

There was also a huge amount of birdlife. Neither animals nor birds seemed afraid of humans.

Fear of man must be an inherited habit.

In England, all birds, even young ones, are afraid of people. But here, they have not yet learned a dread of man.

When *Beagle* left the Galápagos, the crew took several tortoises with them as fresh meat for the next stage of their voyage.

Darwin also took one that he intended to take home with him alive. He called it Harry.

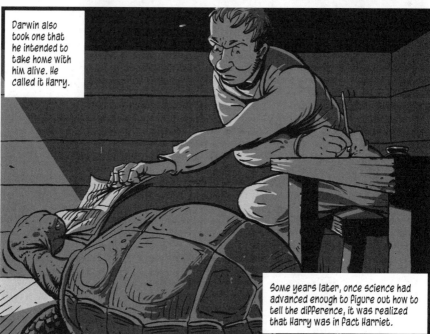

Some years later, once science had advanced enough to figure out how to tell the difference, it was realized that Harry was in fact Harriet.

Darwin gave Harriet to John Wickham, one of the officers on *Beagle* and it seems likely that Wickham took her to Australia with him some years later. Wickham donated the tortoises — one of them called Harriet — to the Botanic Gardens in Brisbane.

Tortoises live an awfully long time. Harriet died in Australia Zoo in Queensland in 2006, 124 years after Charles Darwin.

People who lived on the islands could tell which island each tortoise came from because they all looked different.

The islands were volcanic, and many of the plants and animals were similar to — but not the same as — their counterparts on the mainland of South America. Perhaps their forebears had swum out here, or been carried on driftwood, floating along the ocean currents.

There are no frogs or toads here. They would be killed by salt water.

It was only after he got home that Darwin realized the importance of the things he had seen on the Galápagos.

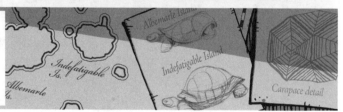

Albemarle Island

Indefatigable Is.

Indefatigable Island

Albemarle Is.

Carapace detail

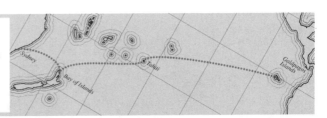

Beagle moved on to Tahiti, New Zealand and then Australia. While she was at Sydney in January 1836, Darwin traveled inland. He was fascinated by the animals in Australia.

How strange the animals are in this country compared to the rest of the world. You might think that two different creators must have been at work. But it cannot be so. One hand has surely worked throughout the universe.

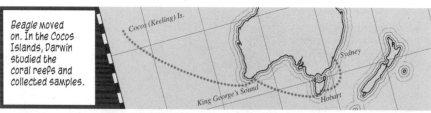

Beagle moved on. In the Cocos Islands, Darwin studied the coral reefs and collected samples.

Cocos (Keeling) Is.

Sydney

Hobart

King George's Sound

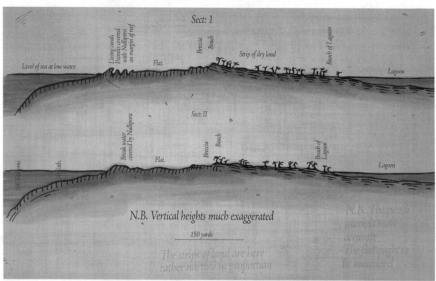

Sect: 1

Level of sea at low water

Living corals
Points covered with Nullipora
on margin of reef

Flat.

Breccia

Beach

Strip of dry land

Beach of Lagoon

Lagoon

Sect: II

Break water
covered by Nullipora

Flat.

Breccia

Beach

Beach of Lagoon

Lagoon

N.B. Vertical heights much exaggerated

150 yards

The strips of land are here rather narrow in proportion

N.B. The pen &
markers more
accurate
The flat ought to
be more level

In Cape Town (now South Africa) he met the great scientist Sir John Herschel, who had set up a huge telescope.

Helena

Mauritius

Cocos (Keeling) Is.

Cape of Good Hope

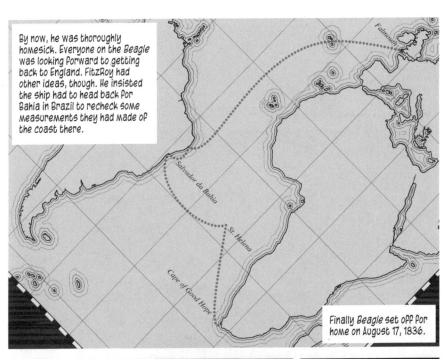

By now, he was thoroughly homesick. Everyone on the *Beagle* was looking forward to getting back to England. FitzRoy had other ideas, though. He insisted the ship had to head back for Bahia in Brazil to recheck some measurements they had made of the coast there.

Finally *Beagle* set off for home on August 17, 1836.

Darwin was seasick most of the way, but happy.

We lie close hauled to the wind, & therefore there is a considerable pitching motion.

BLEURGH

But it is on the road to England!

The *Beagle* put into Falmouth harbor on the evening of Sunday, October 2, 1836, in an autumn storm. It was to be a brief stop before going on to London, but Darwin couldn't wait to get ashore. He was thrilled to be back in England and on dry land.

It took him two days to travel the 250 miles. He arrived home late on the night of October 4th and slipped quietly into bed without waking the rest of the family.

He traveled home to Shrewsbury by horse-drawn coach. He later wrote:

The stupid people on the coach did not seem to think the fields one bit greener than usual … The wide world does not contain so happy a prospect as the rich cultivated land of England.

The first that his father and sisters knew of his return was when he walked into breakfast.

His head has changed shape!

CHARLES!!

Darwin was dizzy with happiness to be home after five years, and everyone was delighted at his safe return. Even the family servants celebrated.

He spent a few days with his family, then rushed off to Cambridge to see his friend Henslow to talk about his adventures. While Darwin had been away, Henslow had been telling other naturalists about the interesting things Darwin was sending back. He had also published some of Darwin's letters. Darwin found himself a celebrity in scientific circles. Other naturalists wanted to meet him, or get their hands on all the interesting things he'd brought home.

Mr. Darwin, I've heard a great deal about you.

He visited his brother in London. Eras was by now "retired"; his health was poor and Robert Darwin had given him enough money to do as he liked.

Eras liked mixing with London's leading thinkers and intellectuals, and of course he introduced his brother to them.

Darwin also went around town visiting museums and naturalists, looking for the best experts to examine his specimens. There were even more to be unloaded when *Beagle* arrived at Woolwych dockyard at the end of her journey.

In all, he brought or sent home 1,529 species preserved in spirits in jars, and 3,907 labeled skins, bones and other "dry" specimens.

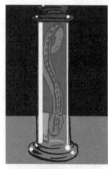

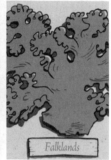

These, along with the notes from his diary and scientific journals, would keep him busy for years to come.

The other thing he brought from *Beagle* was Syms Covington.

Covington had been a cabin boy on *Beagle*, but had become Darwin's assistant, helping him collect, hunt, shoot, skin and stuff things.

Now he became Darwin's servant. He would continue to work for Darwin until 1839.

Darwin became a member of the Geological Society, and gave lectures there.

Many of the world's leading scientists were members, including Charles Lyell, the most famous geologist of the time.

Darwin talked about the geology of South America. He said the continent had been rising over millions of years and that as the landmass moved upward, the ocean floor next to it sunk down.

It appears that the animals on the continent have had to adapt to the changes in climate, altitude and vegetation.

Lyell's view was that as the environment changed, animals died out and were replaced with new species, as directed by God.

Another expert Darwin befriended was the ornithologist (bird expert) John Gould, who examined the skins of various birds Darwin had brought from the Galápagos.

For Mr. Gould

He has contradicted you, Lyell!

But one cannot fault his geology.

Darwin assumed these birds were different species, including finches, blackbirds, wrens and grosbeaks. Gould had startling news:

Gentlemen, these birds are so fascinating that I have set aside all my other work to study them.

They are all, in fact, finches. They form an entirely new group of 12 species, quite different than any ever seen before.

Darwin and Lyell remained good friends.

Each of these finches comes from a different island in the Galápagos.

They are related to finches from the South American mainland.

The most important difference between each is the size and shape of the beak.

The beak of each one is especially suited to the type of seeds or nuts found on each island.

It is as though these birds have all come from the same ancestors, but have all become different on each island.

Darwin was now thinking very hard about "transmutation of species" — the idea that plants and animals did not remain the same, but changed over several generations.

Transmutation was a controversial idea. Few scientists — many of whom, like Henslow, were clergymen — believed in it, and the church was outraged by it.

The church said that living things were created by God, and because God was all-powerful and all-knowing, every creature he created would be perfect. Wouldn't it?

And if things were perfect, they would not need to change. Would they?

In the summer of 1837 Darwin started writing down his thoughts on transmutation in a series of notebooks. He did this in secret, though he shared some thoughts with his brother.

There is other evidence, too — I saw fossil remains of extinct animals that look similar to existing creatures.

Surely the finches and tortoises on the Galápagos are evidence of transmutation.

Their formal resemblance is too striking to be accidental.

And if God had created all animals for the same conditions, why are the creatures on ocean islands all so different?

Why are the animals on the vast island of Australia so different from everywhere else?

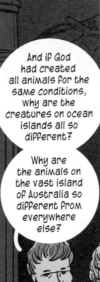

It is much more rational to think that animals arrived on these islands, carried by the winds, or on driftwood, and over thousands of years, they changed.

Perhaps, he thought, all plants and animals had developed from the same ancestors. The French naturalist Lamarck had said this, but Lamarck's idea was that they were getting better all the time.

Think of Lamarck's view of life on Earth as a ladder, with the simplest organisms at the bottom, progressing upward to humans.

Darwin didn't believe this. He thought that life was more like a tree, with different things developing in branches going out in different directions. He made this famous sketch:

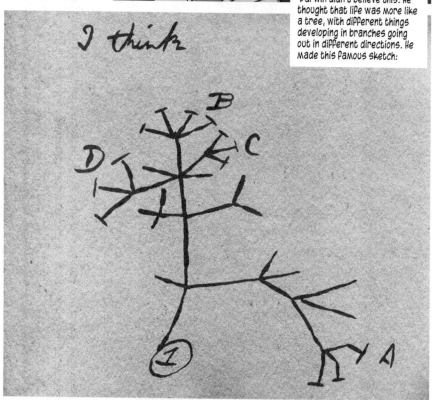

He had been living with his brother, but in March 1837 he moved into his own place at 36 Great Marlborough Street, London.

He also found the time to visit his family in Shropshire, as well as his Uncle Josiah and his Wedgwood cousins. He was paying particular attention to his cousin Emma.

He was starting to think about getting married. He wrote down lists of reasons headed "Marry" and "not Marry":

This is the question:

Not marry OR *marry?*

Freedom to go where one likes

Children (if it please God)

Not forced to visit relatives

Constant companion
(& friend in old age)

Perhaps quarrelling

Charms of music & female chit-chat
— these are good for one's health

Less money for books, etc.

Object to be beloved & played with
— better than a dog anyhow.

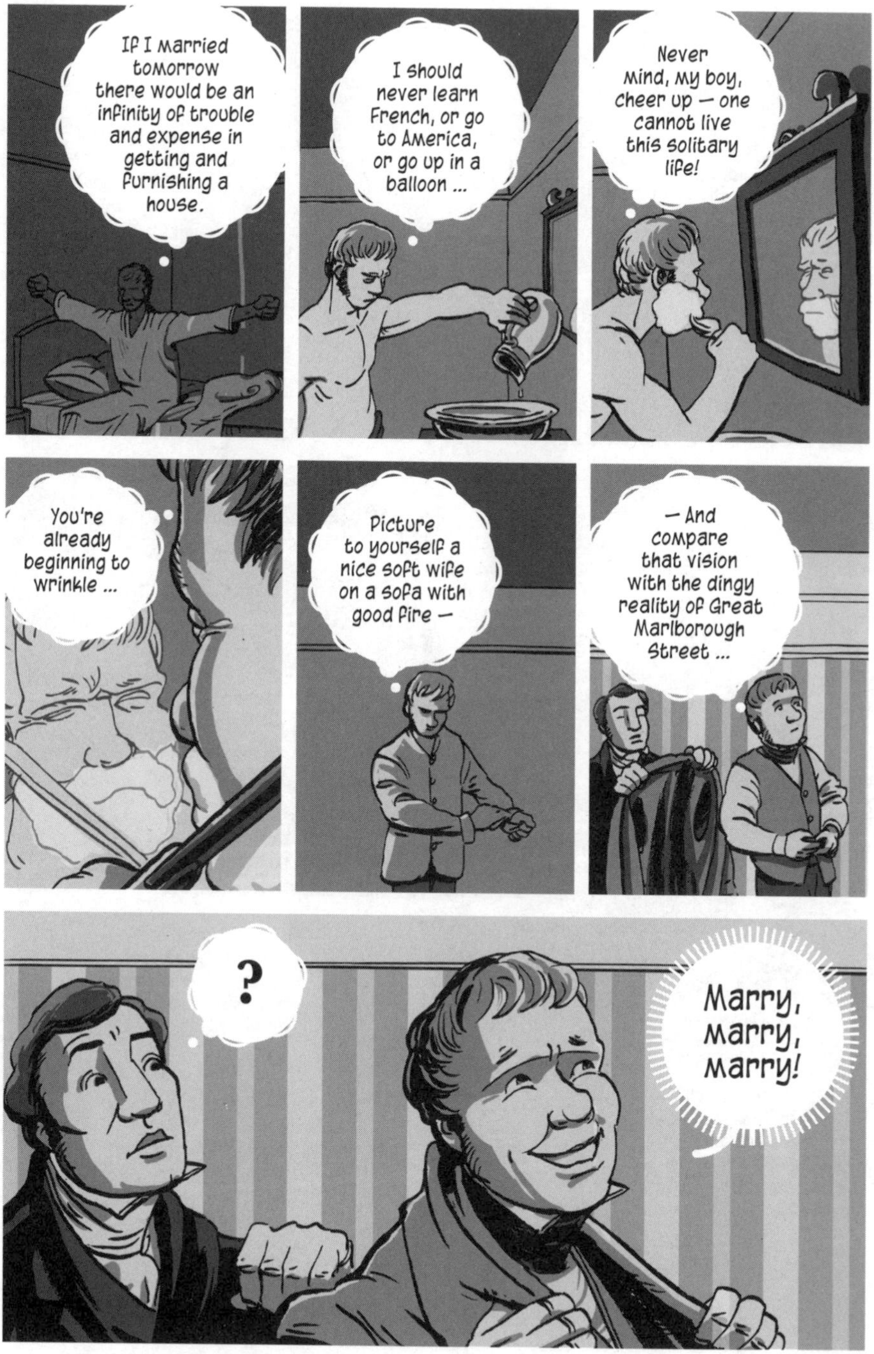
If I married tomorrow there would be an infinity of trouble and expense in getting and furnishing a house.
I should never learn French, or go to America, or go up in a balloon ...
Never mind, my boy, cheer up — one cannot live this solitary life!
You're already beginning to wrinkle ...
Picture to yourself a nice soft wife on a sofa with good fire —
— And compare that vision with the dingy reality of Great Marlborough Street ...
?
Marry, marry, marry!

Visiting his family in Shrewsbury, he told his father about his ideas on transmutation. He also told him he was thinking of marrying his cousin Emma.

One should marry young. It is best for children to have young parents.

If you do not marry soon, you will miss out on much good, pure happiness.

But remember the Wedgwoods are more religious than we Darwins.

If you wish to wed Emma, keep your ideas on transmutation and religion to yourself.

He rode out to the Wedgwood estate to see Emma, but he did not follow his father's advice.

Here we see the humans in their natural habitat.

The male of the species is going through a courtship ritual ...

I believe that nature is not influenced by God, but that it works according to natural laws.

But these laws are laid down by God, are they not?

Courtship ritual?

I thought courtship rituals were all about the male impressing the female with his colorful feathers or showing her how good he is at fighting and hunting.

APE-TV

Perhaps he laid down the laws at the time of the Creation, and then stepped back and no longer intervenes.

This is not the right time to propose.

Well, it's kinda like that in humans. Let me demonstrate...

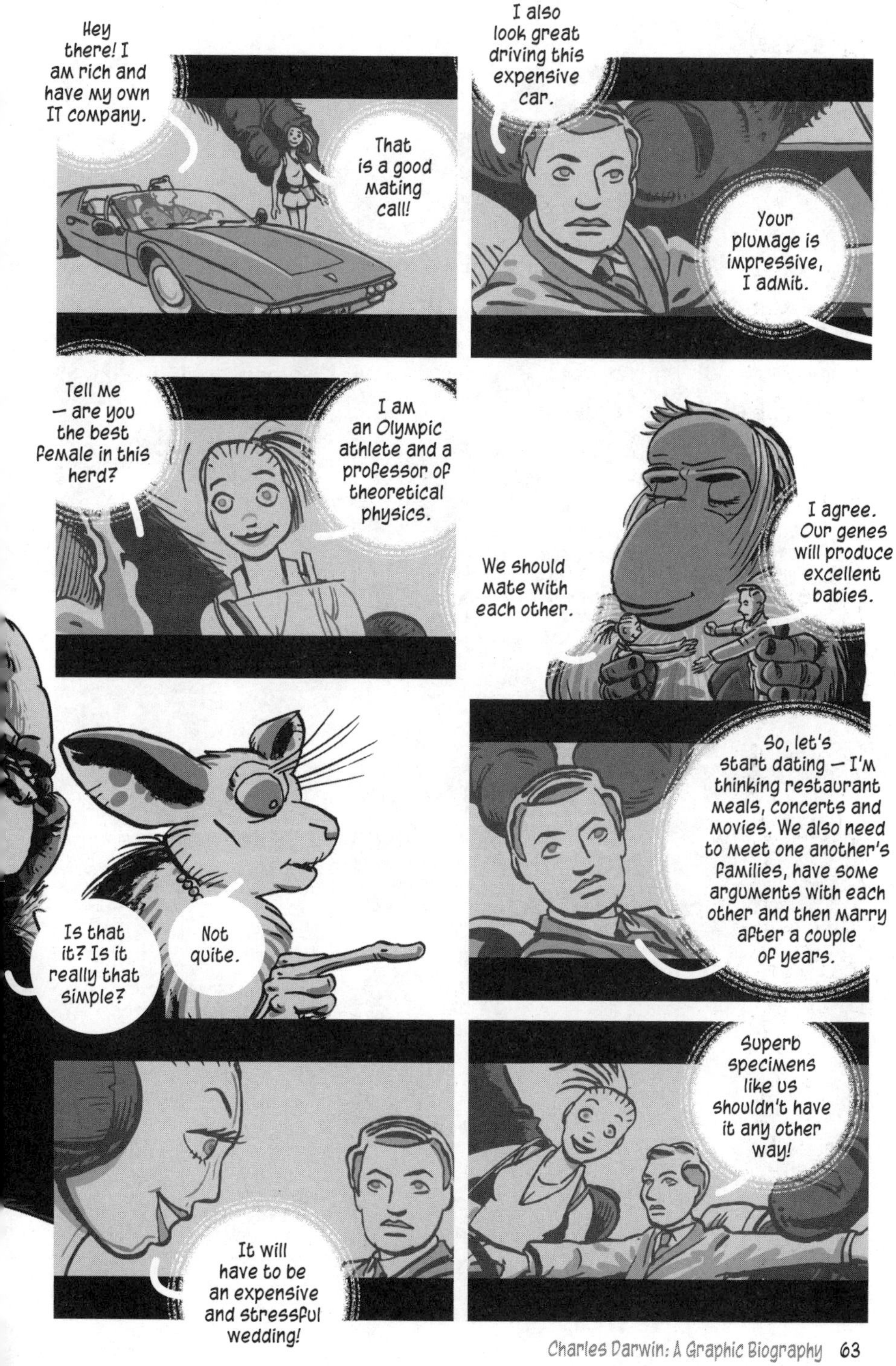

Hey there! I am rich and have my own IT company.
That is a good mating call!
I also look great driving this expensive car.
Your plumage is impressive, I admit.
Tell me — are you the best female in this herd?
I am an Olympic athlete and a professor of theoretical physics.
We should mate with each other.
I agree. Our genes will produce excellent babies.
Is that it? Is it really that simple?
Not quite.
So, let's start dating — I'm thinking restaurant meals, concerts and movies. We also need to meet one another's families, have some arguments with each other and then marry after a couple of years.
It will have to be an expensive and stressful wedding!
Superb specimens like us shouldn't have it any other way!

Back in London Darwin was busy writing books and scientific papers. He also spent a lot of time at London Zoo looking at the facial expressions of baboons and monkeys.

They look almost like humans!

They look almost like monkeys!

Most zoos nowadays are educational and employ scientists who study and try to conserve wildlife.

But in the past they were just places of entertainment.

In the 1830s one of the star attractions at London Zoo was an orangutan called Jenny.

They dressed her in girls' clothes to entertain the crowds. How humiliating and demeaning is that?!!

Right. Time to reenact this famous scene. Jenny, I've got your costume here.

What! NO WAY!! I'll look ridiculous!

Jenny, dearest, you're so very talented that I would hate to have to replace you with another presenter.

Darwin wrote:

The keeper showed her an apple but would not give it her, whereupon she threw herself on her back, kicked and cried, precisely like a naughty child.

She then looked very sulky & after two or three fits of passion the keeper said, "Jenny if you will stop bawling & be a good girl I will give you the apple."

She certainly understood every word of this … She at last succeeded & then got the apple, with which she jumped into an arm-chair & began eating it with the most contented countenance imaginable.

Ha ha ha!

Ow.

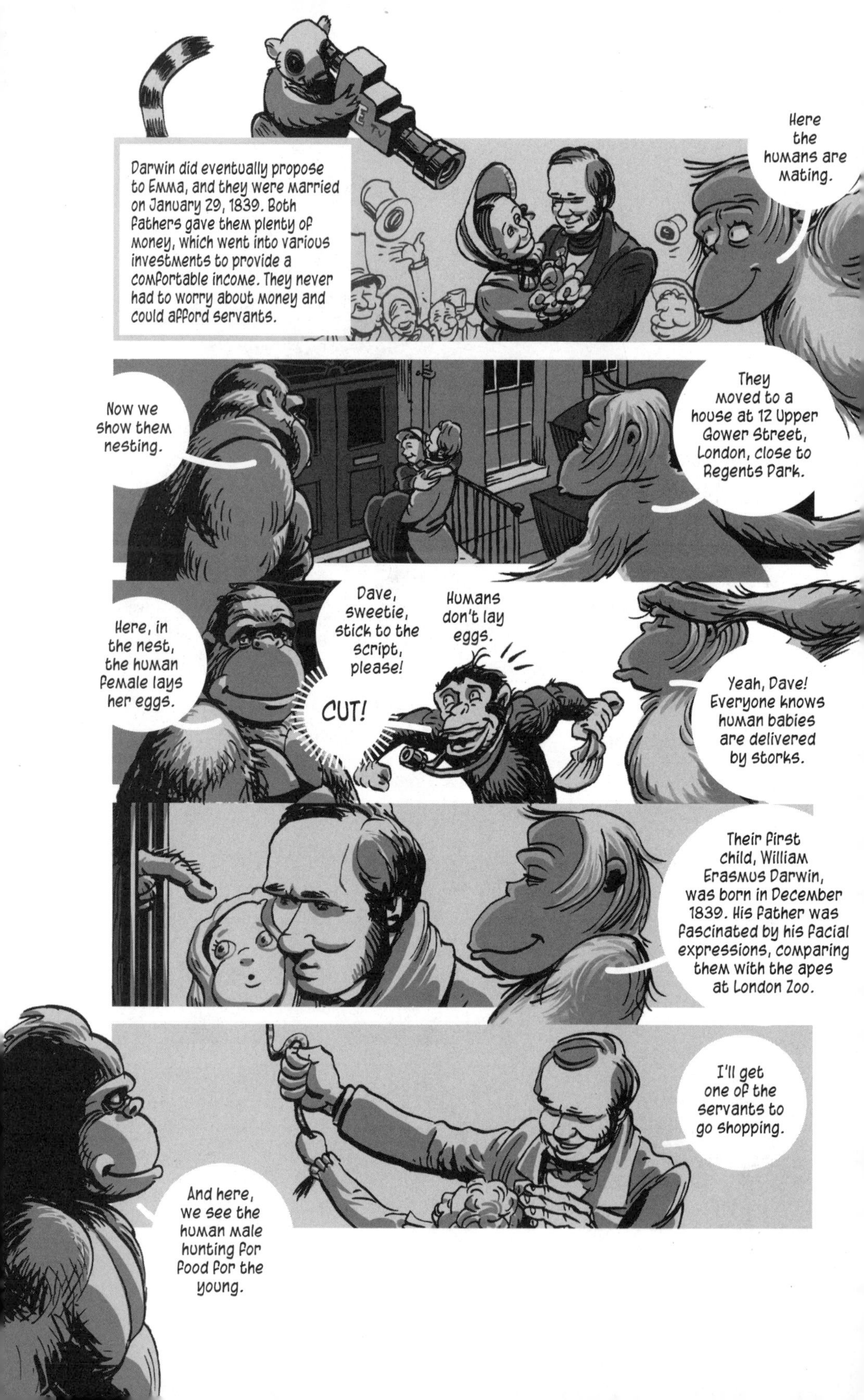

Darwin did eventually propose to Emma, and they were married on January 29, 1839. Both fathers gave them plenty of money, which went into various investments to provide a comfortable income. They never had to worry about money and could afford servants.
Here the humans are mating.
Now we show them nesting.
They moved to a house at 12 Upper Gower Street, London, close to Regents Park.
Here, in the nest, the human female lays her eggs.
CUT!
Dave, sweetie, stick to the script, please!
Humans don't lay eggs.
Yeah, Dave! Everyone knows human babies are delivered by storks.
Their first child, William Erasmus Darwin, was born in December 1839. His father was fascinated by his facial expressions, comparing them with the apes at London Zoo.
I'll get one of the servants to go shopping.
And here, we see the human male hunting for food for the young.

But Darwin's life at this time was not completely happy. He had started to suffer from health problems that would plague him for the rest of his life.

He was regularly struck down by headaches, stomach pains, nausea, weakness, chest pains and belching.

This is no laughing matter!

He could often only work for a few hours each day. He went to Shrewsbury to see the doctor he trusted most — his own father, but Robert Darwin had no idea what was wrong with him.

London was not a healthy place. It was overcrowded, smoky (everyone had coal fires) and dirty. The Thames was an open sewer and diseases like cholera, tuberculosis and typhus killed thousands. This was also a time of great political unrest; there was an economic depression, and starving, angry workers were on the streets. The Darwins decided to get out.

In September 1842 they moved to Down House at Downe in Kent, which in those days was a quiet village. They would live here for the rest of their lives.

Despite his illness and his heavy workload, Darwin was still thinking about transmutation and was very impressed by Thomas Malthus's book *Essay on the Principle of Population*.

Malthus said the human population grows faster than its ability to grow or find enough food. Darwin reckoned the same thing happened in nature. More individuals of each species would be born than could be supported by the food supply. There would be competition among the species for food, a contest in which the strongest would survive and the weakest would die.

In the summer of 1842 he wrote a short outline of what he called "My Theory," and later turned this into a longer 230-page essay.

He left instructions to Emma that if he died suddenly and unexpectedly, it was to be published.

Species change and develop as their environment changes. The individuals of each species best suited to survival in their environment will live, while those that are not will die. And fossils tell us that entire species will sometimes die out.

He kept his theory secret for more than 10 years.

Why?

First, he wasn't absolutely sure about it. If he published his theory and another naturalist proved it was nonsense, his reputation as a scientist would be ruined.

Second, it would anger and upset a lot of his friends, including quite a few naturalists, who still believed that God was somehow involved in nature.

Third, the church would see it as an attack on religion. In 1844, a book called *Vestiges of the Natural History of Creation*, said that everything from the solar system to the Earth, rocks, plants and animals had all developed from other forms. Fossils, it said, were evidence that creatures in the past had died out. They could not possibly have been designed by God, because God would have made them perfect. *Vestiges* said it was ridiculous to believe that God would personally take the trouble to design a new species of shellfish, for example.

In short, this book was making the case for transmutation. It was attacked by the church and by naturalists. Darwin himself thought the science in it was poor. The author – the Scottish journalist and publisher Robert Chambers – chose to remain anonymous because he knew how much trouble it would cause.

Darwin had much better scientific evidence for transmutation, but he decided to keep quiet.

Darwin also disliked the way *Vestiges* was popular with political radicals, atheists (people who don't believe in God) and "freethinkers" who said that beliefs should be based on science and logic, not emotion or religion.

To radicals and freethinkers, the Church of England was a key part of a system that kept aristocrats, landowners and businessmen rich and kept working people poor.

Offending the Church of England was dangerous. Take the case of George Holyoake, for example ...

Holyoake (1817-1906) was on his way to Bristol to become editor of a radical magazine when he gave a talk to working men in Cheltenham. He criticized the church and was arrested and charged with blasphemy and atheism. He was tried by jury for the "crime" of not believing in God, and sentenced to six months in Gloucester prison.

Here he was only fed gruel, bread, rice and potatoes, and was not allowed to read the newspapers his friends sent him. He got into more trouble for refusing to take part in prison prayers. Meanwhile, his wife and children were reduced to poverty and his two-year-old daughter, Madeleine, died as a result.

Darwin wanted nothing to do with atheists and political radicals anyway. He was not interested in politics, but in science.

Darwin's ill health plagued him through all these years, and some of his biographers have suggested that the headaches, nausea, burping, fatigue, etc., were caused by stress and worry over his theory.

Or it might have been something he picked up on his travels. He may have had Chagas disease, which is spread in South America by a bug. Darwin had been bitten by one when traveling in Argentina, writing in his diary at the time:

At night I experienced an attack (for it deserves no less a name) of the Benchuca (Vinchuca) … the great black bug of the Pampas. It is most disgusting to feel soft wingless insects, about an inch long, crawling over one's body. Before sucking they are quite thin but afterwards they become round and bloated with blood.

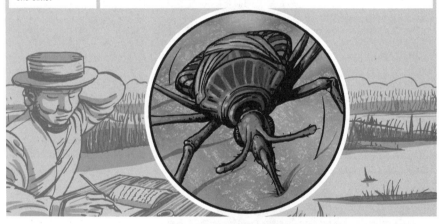

But we really can't be sure what he was suffering from.

At Down House, he hid away from the world, concentrating on his work when he wasn't ill. He even had a mirror outside the window of his study so he could see if there were any visitors approaching. If he didn't want to see them, he would pretend he wasn't in.

He later rented a strip of land near the house where he laid out a path in the shade of the trees — his "Sandwalk" where he would take a stroll every day to think.

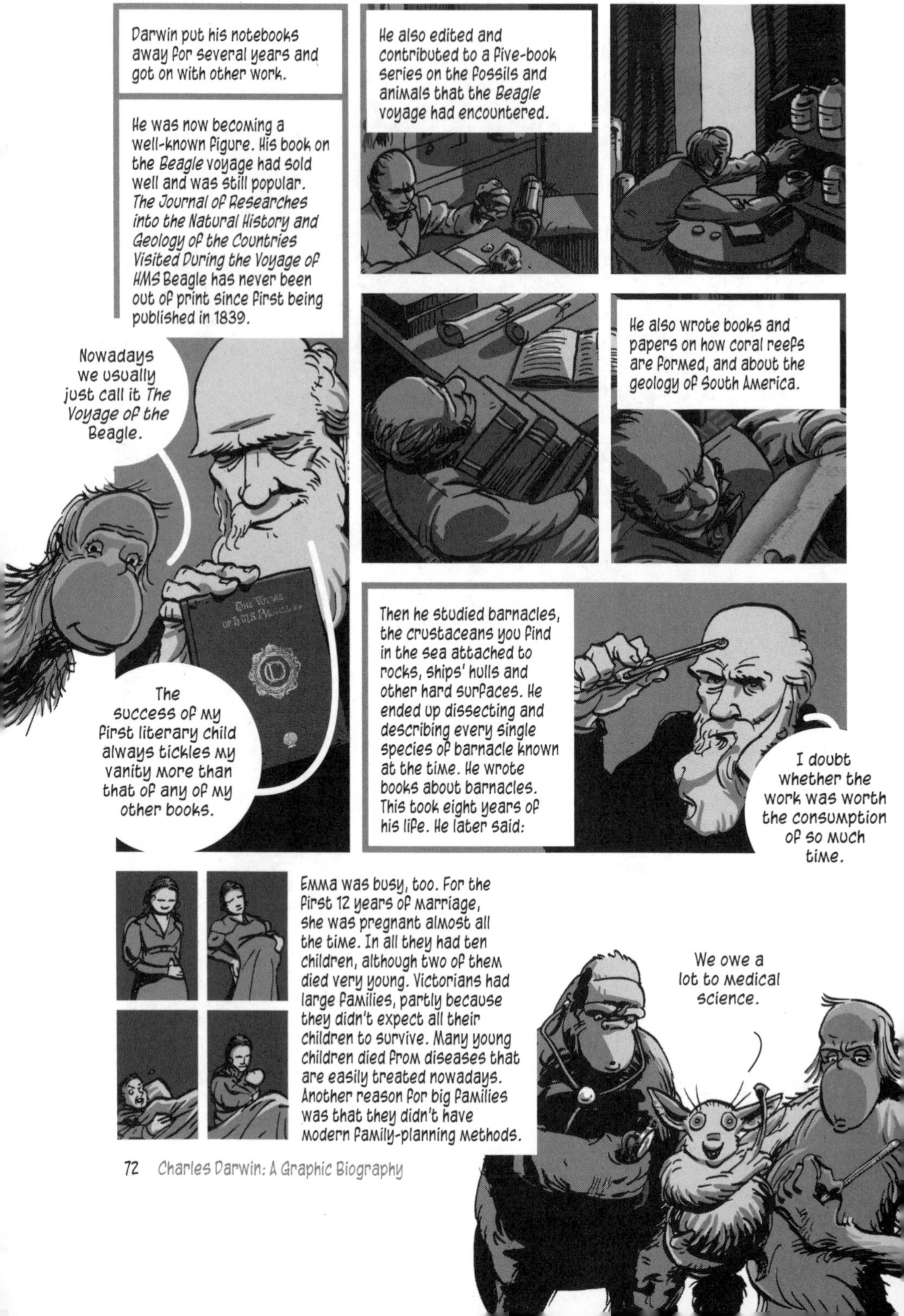

Darwin put his notebooks away for several years and got on with other work.
He was now becoming a well-known figure. His book on the *Beagle* voyage had sold well and was still popular. *The Journal of Researches into the Natural History and Geology of the Countries Visited During the Voyage of HMS* Beagle has never been out of print since first being published in 1839.
Nowadays we usually just call it *The Voyage of the* Beagle.
The success of my first literary child always tickles my vanity more than that of any of my other books.
He also edited and contributed to a five-book series on the fossils and animals that the *Beagle* voyage had encountered.
He also wrote books and papers on how coral reefs are formed, and about the geology of South America.
Then he studied barnacles, the crustaceans you find in the sea attached to rocks, ships' hulls and other hard surfaces. He ended up dissecting and describing every single species of barnacle known at the time. He wrote books about barnacles. This took eight years of his life. He later said:
I doubt whether the work was worth the consumption of so much time.
Emma was busy, too. For the first 12 years of marriage, she was pregnant almost all the time. In all they had ten children, although two of them died very young. Victorians had large families, partly because they didn't expect all their children to survive. Many young children died from diseases that are easily treated nowadays. Another reason for big families was that they didn't have modern family-planning methods.
We owe a lot to medical science.

Darwin was a loving father. Though the children had been told they shouldn't disturb him in his study, he never minded them coming in.

He sometimes got them to help with his work. One visitor once reported that when Darwin was studying earthworms, he had one of the children playing the bassoon to them to see if they could hear.

The Darwin kids didn't always realize their home was different from everyone else's. One of the younger ones once asked a friend:

Where does your father do his barnacles?

It was a terrible blow to both Charles and Emma Darwin when, in 1851, their eldest daughter Annie died of a fever at the age of 10.

She was a most sweet and affectionate child, and I feel sure would have grown into a delightful woman ...

Tears still sometimes come into my eyes, when I think of her sweet ways.

He called it a "bitter and cruel loss" and neither he nor his wife ever completely got over it. This shocking, horrible experience undermined his belief in a loving God.

His health problems continued. When his father died in 1848, Darwin was too ill to get to the funeral in time.

He went to Malvern to see Dr. James Gully, a well-known doctor who specialized in the "water cure." This basically involved spending a lot of time in cold water.

Though Darwin had no confidence in it, he was desperate enough to try anything.

To his surprise, he started feeling much better. When he returned to Down House, he had a shower house built in the garden. It contained a tub in which he would stand every morning.

A 40-gallon tank overhead would release freezing water onto him when he pulled a cord.

Meanwhile, the world was changing. Although the majority of people lived in what we would consider desperate poverty, the political unrest of the 1840s had now faded. Many of the radicals were now considered respectable, and the church and the old aristocracy were being challenged both by industry and by workers' movements.

At the same time, the success of *Vestiges of the Natural History of Creation* showed that many people were starting to question whether all of the Bible was literally true.

Darwin had by now talked about transmutation with a few scientific friends. Aside from Lyell, one of the most important of these was the botanist and explorer Joseph Dalton Hooker.

Hooker was a plant expert, and like Darwin, he had traveled as a naturalist on Royal Navy ships. Darwin had confessed his theories on transmutation to Hooker some years before, saying they were so controversial that he felt as though he was confessing to a murder.

There was also Thomas Huxley, whom he met in the early 1850s. Huxley had also been a Royal Navy naturalist.

Hooker and Huxley didn't agree with him completely, but they encouraged him to publish his theory.

Darwin decided to write a big and very detailed book. Unlike *Vestiges* it would not be aimed at the public, but at his fellow scientists. If he could convince the scientific world of his theory, the rest of the world would follow.

Before he could write it, there was still a lot of work to do.

His studies of barnacles meant that he was now an expert on transmutation — in one type of creature anyway! There are hundreds of different species of barnacle, but all consist of the same basic parts — only the shapes and sizes are different. He worked out how they had evolved from prehistoric crab-like creatures.

He also carried out experiments to prove that seeds could be carried to islands where they might develop into new plant species in isolation from the rest of the world. He took various seeds, soaked them in salt water for weeks at a time and then planted them.

They germinated and grew.

Seeds can be carried to islands on the currents of seas and oceans and will still grow despite being immersed in salt water.

He wrote to naturalists and gardeners asking them for evidence of seeds stuck on birds' feet.

He also dug around in bird droppings looking for seeds they had eaten, and successfully grew these, too, proving that seeds could be carried off in different directions by birds who had eaten them (or the fruits or berries they had been in).

He fed sparrows on seeds and THEN fed the sparrows to an owl and an eagle at London Zoo to test whether or not the seeds survived in the owl and eagle droppings.

I don't mind. It's all for science!

So it was possible for plant life to travel on ocean currents, or attached to the feathers or in the stomachs of birds. Proving this was vital, because without plant life, animals could not survive.

He also became a pigeon fancier. He joined two clubs where pigeon breeders met to discuss their hobby and swap hints and tips. He also wrote letters to pigeon experts and set up his own lofts at Down House — he had about 90 birds by 1856.

He dissected dead pigeons and the embryos from pigeon eggs.

Notice how all the pigeons look different, but their embryos all look the same.

These different birds ALL come from the same ancestors — prehistoric doves.

Darwin's fellow naturalists were bemused by the way he met, and talked to, farmers and working-class animal breeders, and would read farming books and manuals.

They nicknamed him "The Squire."

Farmers and pigeon fanciers interfered with nature, mating birds and animals to get bigger, fatter, more intelligent or more attractive breeds. This was artificial selection.

But now Darwin was ready to write a book about the subject that he had been thinking about for all this time — the way that nature, unassisted by man, creates new species. In other words, NATURAL SELECTION.

But then disaster threatened.

On June 18, 1858, Darwin got a letter from a naturalist named Alfred Russel Wallace.

Wallace was not rich, and paid his way by selling some of his specimens to collectors and other naturalists. He was an important scientist though, discovering over 1,000 previously unknown species, most famously a type of flying frog named after him.

He also realized that there was a geographical boundary that separates species related to Asia from those related to Australia — this is now known as the Wallace Line.

Wallace was traveling in what are nowadays Malaysia and Indonesia, studying nature and collecting specimens.

From his observations and studies, Wallace realized that not only do plants and animals change, but they evolve as well. Like Darwin, he believed in natural selection and now he was writing to Darwin outlining his views.

I never saw a more striking coincidence! If Wallace had my own manuscript, he could not have made a better short summary.

If Wallace published his theory now, he would get all the credit for having the idea first — even though Darwin had spent much of his adult life thinking about natural selection and had much more evidence for it.

So why didn't Darwin just throw away Wallace's letter, tell the world about his theory and grab all the fame?

Because he was a gentleman. Treating other people badly — especially treating a fellow naturalist badly — was unthinkable.

I would rather burn my whole book than Wallace or any other man should think I had behaved in a paltry spirit!

In the end, Darwin's friend Lyell came up with the solution. Darwin and Wallace should announce their theory together.

So the theory of natural selection was first announced to the world by Lyell and Hooker at a meeting in London of the Linnean Society* on July 1, 1858.

*Linnean Society of London, still one of the world's leading organizations for biologists and botanists, is named after the Swedish biologist Carl Linnaeus, who pioneered the system of naming and classifying different species.

Darwin himself was not there. He and the family were mourning the loss of their youngest child, Charles Waring Darwin, who had just died of scarlet fever at age two.

The joint Darwin/Wallace paper was published as

On the Tendency of Species to form Varieties; and on the Perpetuation of Varieties and Species by Natural Means of Selection. By CHARLES DARWIN, Esq., F.R.S., F.L.S., & F.G.S., and ALFRED WALLACE, Esq. Communicated by Sir CHARLES LYELL, F.R.S., F.L.S., and J.D. HOOKER, Esq., M.D., V.P.R.S., F.L.S., &c.

Wallace didn't know any of this. He was still away on his travels. When he did hear about it, he was very happy, because Darwin knew much more than he did. Darwin was hugely relieved that Wallace didn't think he'd stolen the credit for the idea.

Wallace is too modest, and admirably free from envy or jealousy. He must be a good fellow.

The two men later became good friends. When Wallace published his hugely popular book about his travels, *The Malay Archipelago* (1869), he dedicated it to Darwin.

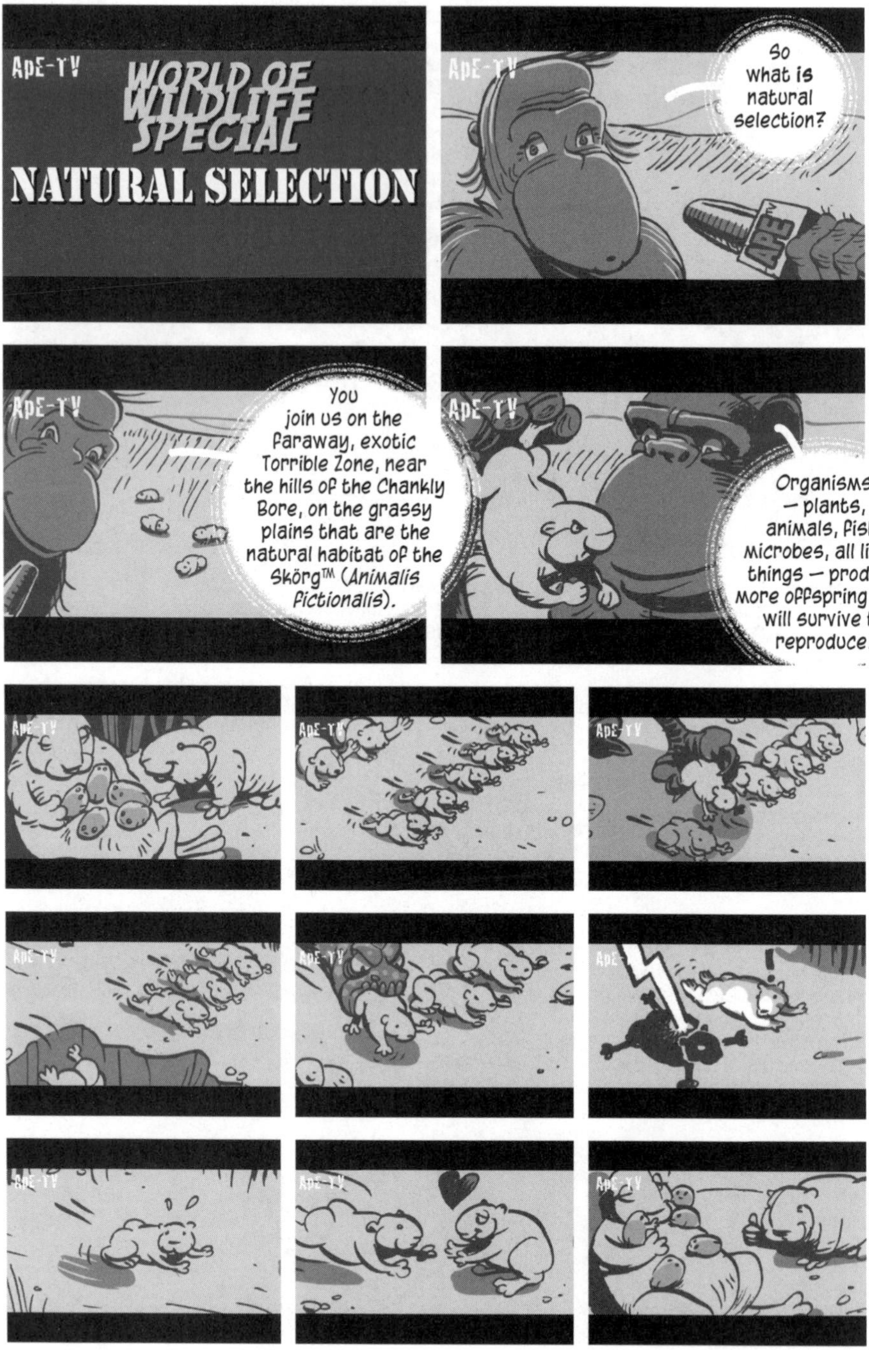
ApE-TV
WORLD OF WILDLIFE SPECIAL
NATURAL SELECTION
So what is natural selection?
APE TV
You join us on the faraway, exotic Torrible Zone, near the hills of the Chankly Bore, on the grassy plains that are the natural habitat of the Skörg™ (*Animalis fictionalis*).
Organisms — plants, animals, fish, microbes, all living things — produce more offspring than will survive to reproduce.

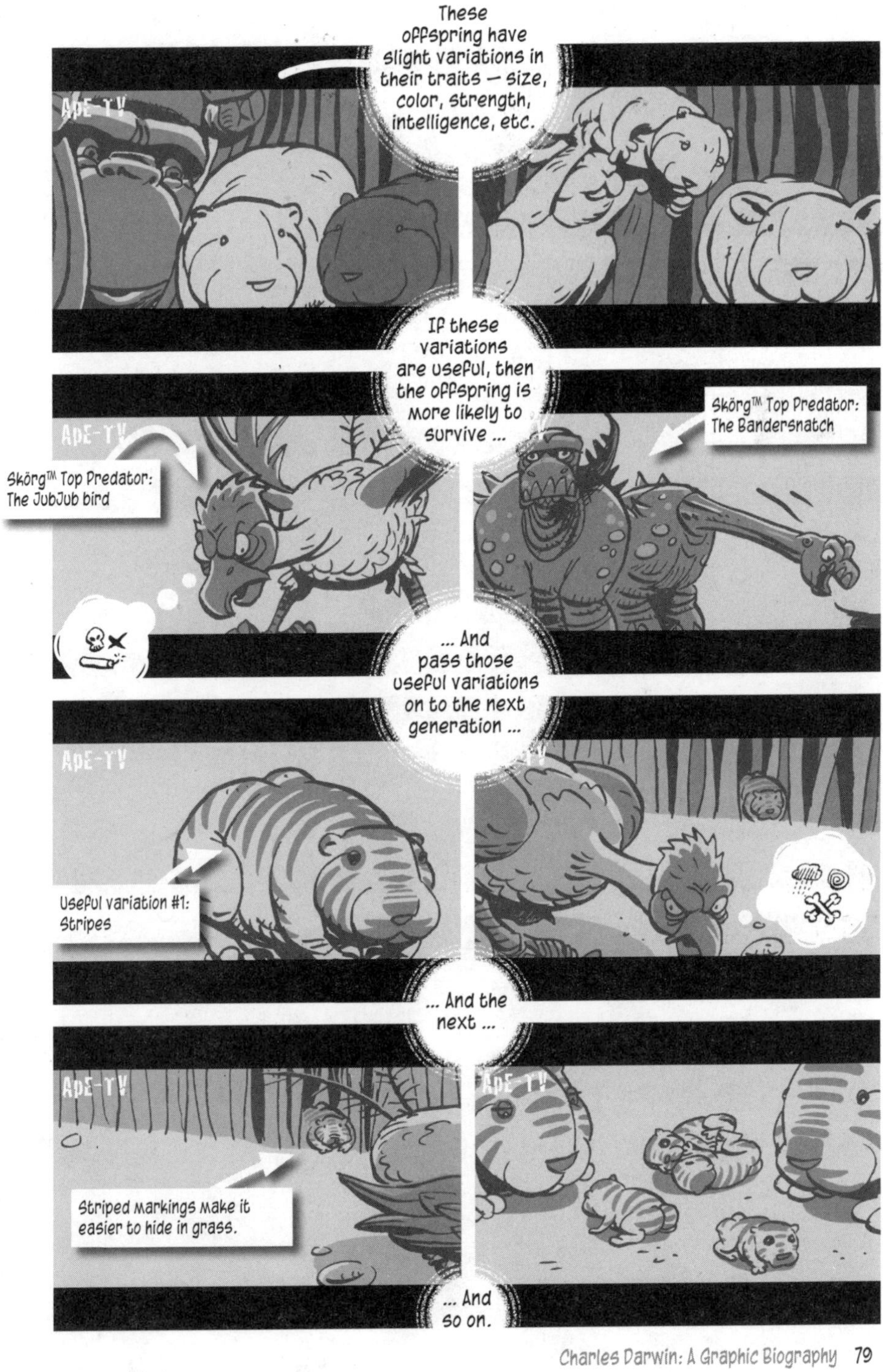
These offspring have slight variations in their traits — size, color, strength, intelligence, etc.
ApE-TV
If these variations are useful, then the offspring is more likely to survive ...
Skörg™ Top Predator: The JubJub bird
Skörg™ Top Predator: The Bandersnatch
... And pass those useful variations on to the next generation ...
Useful variation #1: Stripes
... And the next ...
Striped markings make it easier to hide in grass.
... And so on.

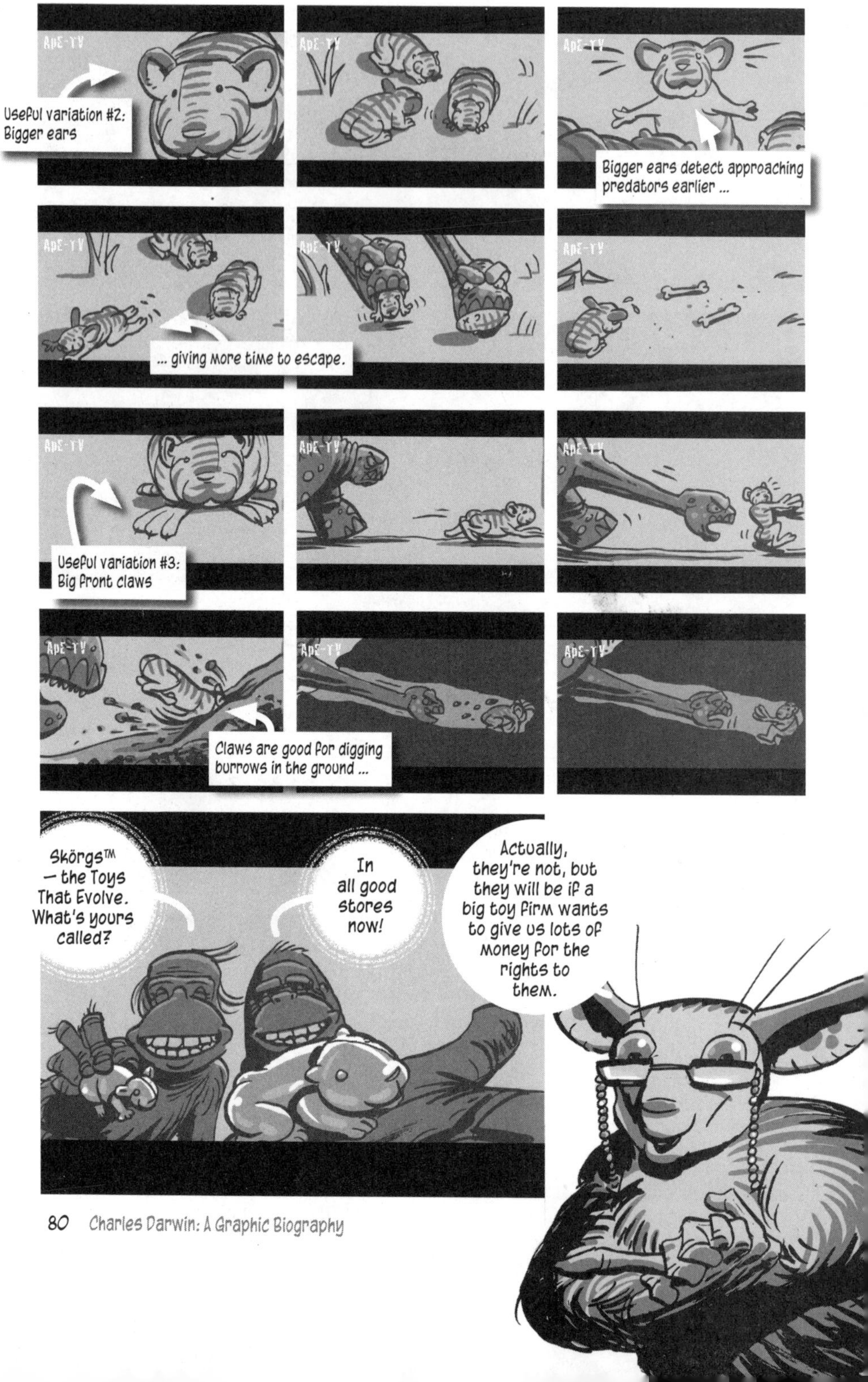
Ape-TV
Useful variation #2:
Bigger ears
Bigger ears detect approaching predators earlier ...
... giving more time to escape.
Useful variation #3:
Big front claws
Claws are good for digging burrows in the ground ...
Skörgs™ — the Toys That Evolve. What's yours called?
In all good stores now!
Actually, they're not, but they will be if a big toy firm wants to give us lots of money for the rights to them.

Darwin and Wallace's paper mentioned things like eagle and cat claws, saying:

Those always survived longest which had the greatest facilities for seizing their prey.

Or the giraffe, which got its long neck because those with longer necks than the rest could reach higher to get more food.

Or the colors of insects: those that matched the color of the soil, leaves or tree trunks they lived on would survive the longest.

These differences build up over time and gradually lead to entirely new types of life — new species.

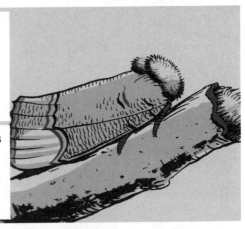

A species is a group of animals or plants that can breed with one another; a new species is formed when two populations build up so many differences that they can no longer interbreed and produce fertile offspring.

So for instance, although horses and donkeys are separate species, you can mate a male donkey with a female horse and you'll get a mule. But mules are sterile — they can't have offspring of their own.

You might get new species when two populations become separated geographically — for instance if they become isolated on islands or when a river changes course or earthquake creates hills or mountains.

Darwin now gave up on writing a huge book for scientists and wrote a smaller book for the general public, completing it in nine months despite his usual health problems.

When he was finished, he felt "as weak as a child."

It was published in November 1859; 1,250 copies were printed and sold out quickly, despite its relatively high price — more than a week's pay for most people.

On the Origin of Species by Means of Natural Selection, or the Preservation of Favoured Races in the Struggle for Life — usually just known as Origin of Species — brought what we now call Darwin's theory of evolution to the attention of the public.

ON

THE ORIGIN OF SPECIES

BY MEANS OF NATURAL SELECTION,

OR THE

PRESERVATION OF FAVOURED RACES IN THE STRUGGLE
FOR LIFE.

BY CHARLES DARWIN, M.A.,

FELLOW OF THE ROYAL, GEOLOGICAL, LINNEAN, ETC. SOCIETIES;
AUTHOR OF 'JOURNAL OF RESEARCHES DURING H.M.S. BEAGLE'S VOYAGE
ROUND THE WORLD.'

LONDON:
JOHN MURRAY, ALBEMARLE STREET
1859.

It caused a sensation.

A second edition was printed a few months later, and there were four more in Darwin's lifetime. It was translated into the main European languages within a few years.

When Darwin heard of working men in Lancashire pitching in to buy a copy to share, he insisted on a cheaper new edition; the sixth (1872) was printed in much smaller type so that the price could be halved.

Some Christians condemned it but others agreed with it, saying it was perfectly possible to believe in God and accept natural selection.

God, as the Christian writer and historian Charles Kingsley put it ...

... has created primal forms capable of self-development into all forms needful.

Meaning God had created primitive life-forms, but had programmed them with the ability to evolve and develop.

Darwin himself never speculated about how life had originated, only how it evolved. Although Annie's death had shaken him, he never rejected religion completely. He was a member of his local church, giving it money and helping with its charities.

I have never been an atheist in the sense of denying the existence of a God. I think that agnostic would be the more correct description of my state of mind.

The word "agnostic" — from the Greek meaning "without knowledge" — was coined by Huxley to describe those who, like Darwin and himself, don't follow any religion, but don't completely reject it either.

Nobody can *prove* God exists, and nor can anyone prove he does *not* exist.

Darwin took little part in public discussions of natural selection because of his poor health — and because he hated arguments. Huxley, however, loved them. He called himself "Darwin's Bulldog."

The Bulldog's most famous outing was on June 30, 1860, at a meeting of the British Association for the Advancement of Science at Oxford University Museum Library.

Up to 1,000 people attended a debate on natural selection, with various distinguished speakers both attacking and defending Darwin's theory.

One of those against Darwin was Samuel Wilberforce, Bishop of Oxford.

Soapy Sam:— "WOULD MR. HUXLEY CARE TO TELL US WHETHER HE IS DESCENDED FROM MONKEYS ON HIS GRANDFATHER'S OR GRANDMOTHER'S SIDE?"

Mr. Huxley:— "I WOULD RATHER BE DESCENDED FROM AN APE THAN FROM A MAN WHO USES HIS GREAT INFLUENCE AND LEARNING JUST TO BRING RIDICULE INTO AN IMPORTANT SCIENTIFIC DISCUSSION."

Darwin hadn't said *anything* about man being descended from monkeys in *Origin*. He hadn't written about human evolution at all, but the logic of natural selection was that man is indeed related to monkeys.

According to some accounts, the meeting ended in uproar, with one lady fainting, while a man wandered around holding up a huge Bible and shouting:

The book! The book!

It was Captain FitzRoy. As a devout Christian, he refused to accept natural selection, and blamed himself for taking Darwin on the voyage that had resulted in the theory.

For evidence of evolution, Darwin pointed to fossils, the preserved remains of ancient creatures and plants that are virtually all now extinct.

One of the main criticisms of Darwin's theory was that fossils don't tell the whole story of evolution. In Darwin's time there were few fossilized animals that showed "intermediate types" — creatures that were in between one type and another, which would show evolution in action.

150 years later, we have many more fossils, and there are now plenty of these "missing links." But they were turning up even when he was alive. The discovery in 1863 of a lizard-bird fossil in Germany was hugely exciting. Called "Archaeopteryx" this creature looked like a bird but had lizard features, including teeth and a bony tail.

There was also "adaptive radiation" — different creatures with changes in characteristics from a single original species. The Galápagos finches all came from the same ancestors, but diversified as they evolved different types of beaks on their different islands.

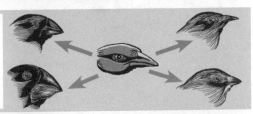

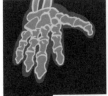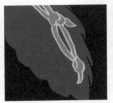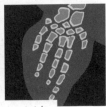

And look at the bones of a human hand, a bird's wings, a cat's paw and a whale's fin. They are all the same basic structure, but have simply evolved differently.

Another problem for Darwin was the question of how complex organs are formed. The example that was usually used is the eye. How could something so sophisticated, have just evolved through natural selection?

The human eye is not as good as it could be because there are blood vessels on the surface of the retina, instead of running beneath it. These blood vessels can leak or impair vision. So if humans were made by an "intelligent designer," like Paley's watchmaker, the eye would be more efficient.

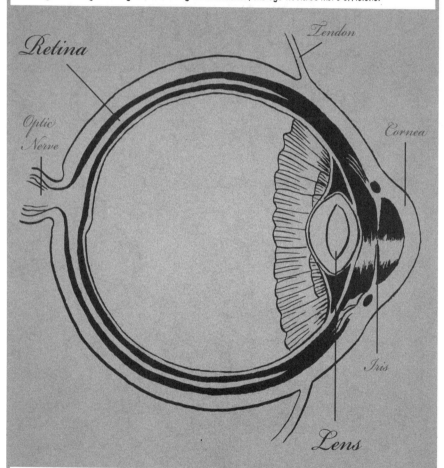

Many scientists now think the eye evolved from a light-sensitive spot on a prehistoric animal's skin, which then went through various changes. The light-sensitive patch developed in a dent in the skin, then into a hole through which light entered through a small slit, then the light-sensitive patch evolved into a retina, then a lens formed at the front of the eye ...

Sounds fantastic? Well, there are sensors and "eyes" from every stage in this sequence in existing living animals. This whole range of primitive eyes shows that complicated eyes like ours can indeed evolve.

Darwin's other big problem was that he had no idea *how* natural selection happens. What causes the changes – the longer necks, the bigger claws, the camouflage colors, etc. – that enable evolution.

He put forward a suggestion inspired by Lamarck – each parent has tiny particles he called "gemmules" that circulate in the body and are mingled when the parents reproduce, giving their offspring a resemblance to both parents. He was wrong.

During Darwin's lifetime, an obscure Austrian monk called Gregor Mendel (1822-1884) was experimenting with growing peas.

He proved that there were definite patterns to the way in which traits are inherited by offspring.

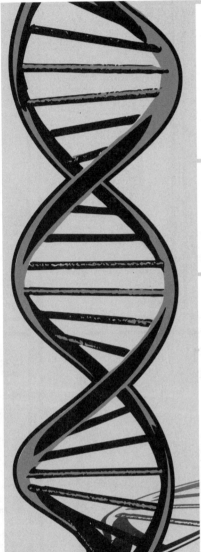

By the early 20th century, Mendel's work, along with the invention of more powerful microscopes, and the work of other scientists, particularly the German August Weissmann (1834-1914) paved the way for genetics – the science of how organisms inherit their characteristics.

Every single living organism on the planet (except possibly certain types of virus) contains DNA. The DNA and the genetic information on it is the plan for reproducing the species.

Variations happen when there are mutations, little changes, in the genes. Most evolutionary change can be explained by mutations – tiny changes – in the DNA as it is passed down the generations.

If two species are closely related, their DNA is very similar, and modern scientists use these similarities to work out our evolutionary relationships. Some 96 percent of human DNA is identical to chimpanzee DNA, for instance. And humans and chimps are more closely related to one another than either is to gorillas.

Darwin's pioneering work on natural selection, plus the science of genetics, came together in what biologists call the Modern Synthesis.

Everything alive today, and everything that has ever lived, is a member of the same big family, carrying the same set of chemical blueprints for reproduction. Every single living thing on the planet is related, just as Darwin predicted when he drew his tree of life.

After *Origin*, Darwin was as busy as ever. He devoted a lot of time to studying plants, which were just as important for his theories as animals.

After watching insects pollinating orchids in the fields around Torquay, which he visited on holiday with his daughter Henrietta, he gave up breeding pigeons and took up raising orchids instead. He wanted to see how orchids used their intricate petal designs to attract bees and moths to their pollen.

In his 1862 book *On the Various Contrivances by which British and Foreign Orchids are Fertilised by Insects* he said that the complicated shapes of orchid flowers were not simply beautiful, or created to please humans, but were adaptations to help reproduction. These complicated shapes existed to ensure they were cross-pollinated by insects.

Remember the *Angraecum sesquipedale* of Madagascar and the moth with the 10-inch proboscis?

Darwin was also interested in plants that eat insects — some of his experiments involved feeding them cooked meat from the dinner table — and wrote a book on them (*Insectivorous Plants*, 1875).

He also studied domestic pigeons, ducks and geese for a book on how breeders and horticulturists modify species.

He then turned to human evolution. Humans have evolved just like every other animal, but he had not dealt with it in *Origin* because it was a big subject on its own, and because it was so controversial.

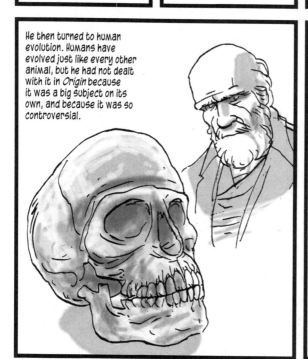

To many Christians, it was outrageous to suggest that humans are part of nature, related to animals and plants. To them, humans were special and created by God with two things animals don't have — morality and reason. Humans have a sense of right and wrong, and the ability to think.

Darwin's answer was that humans have survived because their intelligence is more highly evolved. And morality enables humans to live together and look after one another. Trusting one another and treating each other fairly (which they do most of the time) helps the human race to survive.

His book *The Descent of Man, and Selection in Relation to Sex* (1871) was a great success.

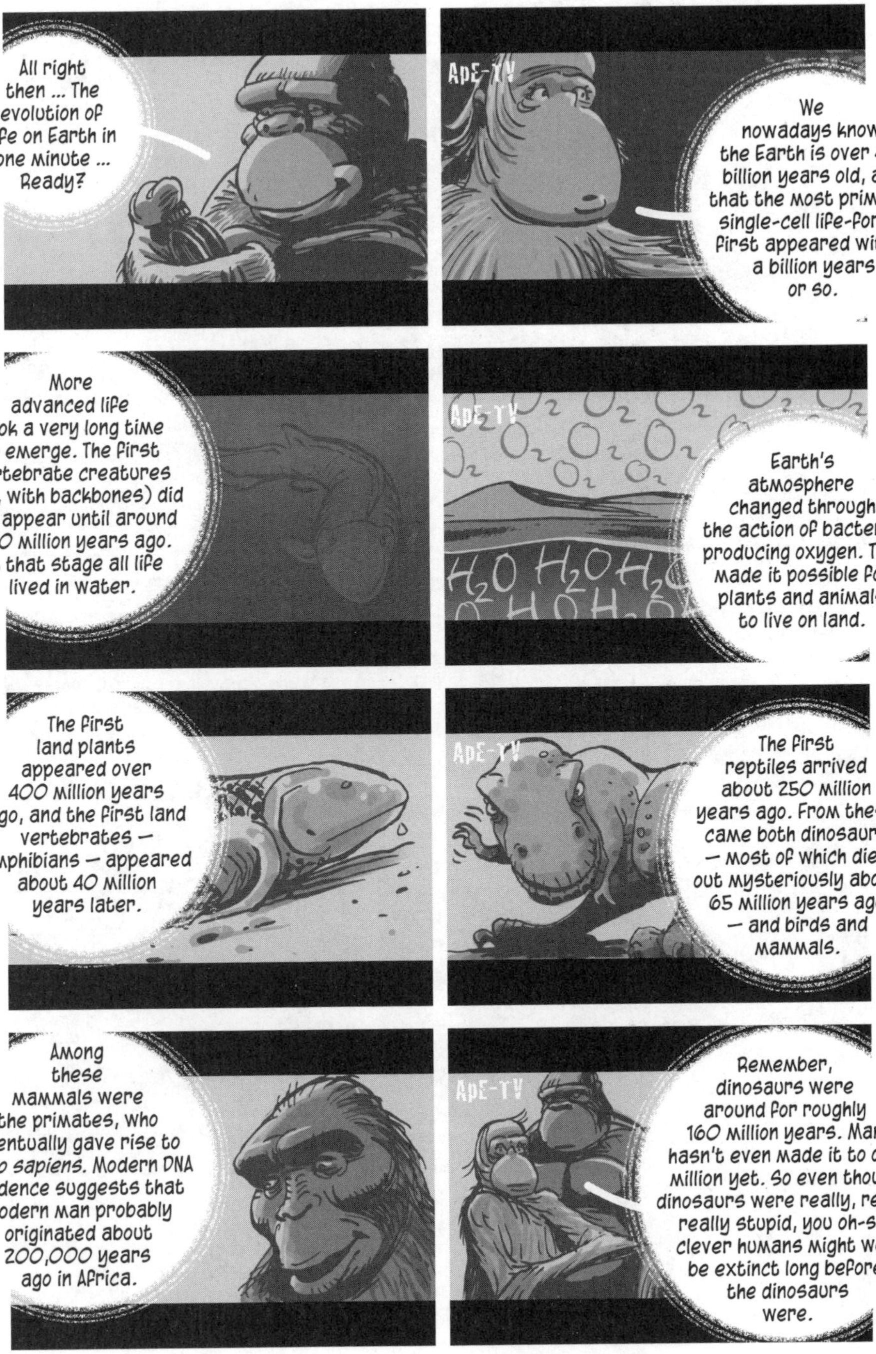
All right then ... The evolution of life on Earth in one minute ... Ready?
We nowadays know the Earth is over 4.5 billion years old, and that the most primitive single-cell life-forms first appeared within a billion years or so.
More advanced life took a very long time to emerge. The first vertebrate creatures (i.e., with backbones) did not appear until around 500 million years ago. At that stage all life lived in water.
Earth's atmosphere changed through the action of bacteria producing oxygen. This made it possible for plants and animals to live on land.
The first land plants appeared over 400 million years ago, and the first land vertebrates — amphibians — appeared about 40 million years later.
The first reptiles arrived about 250 million years ago. From these came both dinosaurs — most of which died out mysteriously about 65 million years ago — and birds and mammals.
Among these mammals were the primates, who eventually gave rise to *Homo sapiens*. Modern DNA evidence suggests that modern man probably originated about 200,000 years ago in Africa.
Remember, dinosaurs were around for roughly 160 million years. Man hasn't even made it to one million yet. So even though dinosaurs were really, really, really stupid, you oh-so-clever humans might well be extinct long before the dinosaurs were.

Evolution is usually a very slow process, but there are times when you can see it in action, moving surprisingly quickly.

One famous example is the insecticide DDT (dichlorodiphenyltrichlo-roethane). DDT was used in many places to kill mosquitoes in the 1940s and 1950s because the insects carry malaria. But mosquitoes have a rapid life cycle. So even though DDT killed most of them at first, some survived and passed their immunity on to their descendants.

Within a few years they were as big a problem as before.

Or take antibiotics. These medicines, used to treat certain bacterial diseases, have saved countless lives.

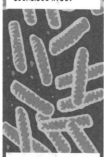

But misuse and over-use of anti-biotics in medicine and farming means that bacteria are evolving resistance to them.

It's now becoming difficult to treat some diseases.

Then there are viruses. They're much smaller than bacteria and can reproduce and change with astonishing speed. This is why infections such as HIV and flu are difficult to cure. One big worry at the moment is H5N1 avian influenza — "bird flu." It can spread from birds to people, but not between people.

But if it swaps genes with another virus that enables it to spread between humans, there might be a worldwide pandemic that could potentially kill millions.

Humans have ways of trying to prevent or delay evolution among tiny critters. In England, the public health authorities gave schoolchildren special shampoos to kill head lice. By the 1980s they thought that every kid's head would soon be lice-free.

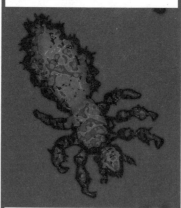

They reckoned without evolution, though; the surviving lice passed on their immunity. Nowadays, school districts rotate shampoos every few years in the hope that lice won't have the time to develop a critical level of immunity.

Evolution can operate amazingly quickly even among larger creatures.

Take the cane toads. (Actually, in Australia, they wish you would take the cane toads — all of them.) Cane toads are native to South America, but were brought to Australia in the 1930s in an attempt to control beetles eating sugarcane crops. Cane toads thrived in their new home and are now a huge pest. The toads moving to new areas across the continent have developed longer legs than the toads still living in the places where they're already established.

Native Australian red-bellied black snakes at first thought cane toads might be a tasty meal. But a poison on the cane toad's skin killed the snakes that ate them.

Now the snakes have evolved a resistance to the toad toxin — and in any case they've learned not to eat them! That's evolution in action.

Remember those finches on the Galápagos Islands? The birds that inspired Darwin's early ideas on transmutation?

Married couple Peter and Rosemary Grant, evolutionary biologists at Princeton University, started visiting the Galápagos in the 1970s to study them. They found that a finch that had moved from one island to another had developed into a new species in less than 30 years.

Darwin had long been interested in human and animal expressions, and in 1872 published *The Expression of the Emotions in Man and Animals*. It was popular, partly because it was one of the first books to be illustrated with photographs. It looked at how animals experience traces of human emotions.

Darwin's health improved as he got older, and he was now world-famous. Scientific societies awarded him honors and medals, and in 1877, Cambridge University awarded him an honorary doctorate.

Important people visited him. British prime minister William Gladstone paid him a visit at Down House in 1877.

In his later years, Darwin devoted himself to studying earthworms, and how they shifted stupendous quantities of earth over years, thus helping life evolve and transforming the soil.

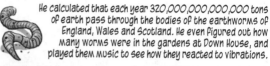

He calculated that each year 320,000,000,000,000 tons of earth pass through the bodies of the earthworms of England, Wales and Scotland. He even figured out how many worms were in the gardens at Down House, and played them music to see how they reacted to vibrations.

Do you know there's an average of 53,767 worms in every acre?

You hum it and I'll play it.

From the middle of 1881 he started to suffer from heart problems and his health deteriorated.

He had a number of heart attacks over several months and died at Down House on April 19, 1882, at age 73.

On April 26, 1882, Darwin was buried in Westminster Abbey, close to the monument to Sir Isaac Newton. Eight men carried his coffin. These included Hooker and Huxley, two dukes, a lord, a senior church official, and the United States ambassador James Russell Lowell.

Although he had wanted to be buried at the churchyard at Downe, the politicians and scientists wanted something more grand for one of the most important Englishmen who had ever lived.

Emma stayed at Down House because she was too upset.

Darwin's ideas were fought over in his lifetime, and they have been fought over ever since. Quite early on, they were twisted into what was called "social Darwinism."

After reading *Origin of Species* the philosopher Herbert Spencer (1820-1903) said that nature was all a matter of

Survival of the fittest.

And social Darwinism applied "survival of the fittest" to human beings.

Some social Darwinists said the poor should not be helped because they would only breed and weaken a healthy society. Social Darwinism was even applied to entire nations — the strongest would prosper, while the weak would be wiped out. This idea was partly behind the huge buildup of armies and navies in Europe that led to the First World War.

The biologist Sir Francis Galton — a distant relative of Darwin's — said the evolution of the human race would be best served if the "best" people were encouraged to have more children. Galton's ideas on what he called "eugenics" — and indeed the whole idea of social Darwinism — was taken to extremes by the Nazis.

Darwin himself would have been appalled. He was interested in science, not politics, but he said that sympathy and care for the weak were an essential part of man's nature, and that neglecting them would be evil.

When most people use the term "survival of the fittest" they're misunderstanding what Darwin actually meant.

The species that evolution favors, according to Darwin are not necessarily "fittest" in the sense of being the strongest, fastest or most intelligent.

The "fittest" are the species best adapted to their particular environment.

Since Darwin's time, scientists have made many more discoveries about evolution. They're still making them.

The theory is still incomplete. There are many things we still don't understand, but that's what science is all about — using observation and experiments to find out more about the world and the wider universe around us.

Not everyone agrees with evolution. Some Christian fundamentalists believe that the Creation Story, as related in the Old Testament, is mostly or completely factually true.

You'll often hear some people say that evolution is

"Only a theory."

In science, the word "theory" does not mean a hunch, or a guess. The scientific word for hunch or guess is "hypothesis."

A theory is a hypothesis that has been tested by observations and experiments.

Evolution is a theory that has passed more than 150 years' worth of tests.

The point is that evolution can be tested.

If you come up with a better theory and can produce enough evidence for it, then you can prove evolution is wrong. That's what science is all about.

As one famous scientist said:

Nothing in biology makes sense except in the light of evolution.

Ukranian-born biologist Theodosius Dobzhansky (1900-1975) became a US citizen in 1937 and considered himself a Christian.

The Catholic Church accepts evolution, but says that what makes humans special in the eyes of God is that they have souls.

In England, the Anglican Church, which Darwin was once going to join, accepts evolution, too. Its associated church in the United States, the Episcopal Church, made a special announcement in 2006 saying that evolutionary theory does not conflict with Christian faith.

Accepting the theory of evolution doesn't make you an atheist. Many religious people believe in what's called theistic evolution or Christian Darwinism.

This is the concept that God, the intelligent designer, created the universe in such a way that everything would evolve naturally. That is, God set everything in motion and then stood back to let evolution follow its course.

Many scientists — perhaps even most — are religious themselves. For example, the American geneticist Francis Collins, is a devout Christian. Collins led the Human Genome Project studying the genetic makeup of humans. This important research is giving us huge advances in medical science.

He said: Evolution by descent from a common ancestor is clearly true. If there was any lingering doubt about the evidence from the fossil record, the study of DNA provides the strongest possible proof of our relatedness to all other living things.

Modern-day molecular biology — the study of life at the smallest level — is providing evidence for evolution that people in Darwin's time never even dreamed of.

Scientists are constantly finding out more and more about the nature of DNA and the workings of organisms at a molecular level. By studying the similarities and differences in these molecules, scientists gradually are building a comprehensive picture of the evolution of life on Earth, even of things for which there is no evidence in the fossils uncovered so far.

And if (or when!) humankind finds evidence of life on other planets, the very first thing we'll do is look to see if it has DNA that looks anything like that of life on Earth.

That's all we've got time for, I'm afraid.

But isn't it nice to know that we're all related to one another?

Does that mean I have to buy birthday presents for everyone?

You never buy birthday presents for anyone.

Charles Darwin: A Graphic Biography 95

It is interesting to contemplate an entangled bank, clothed with many plants of many kinds, with birds singing on the bushes, with various insects flitting about, and with worms crawling through the damp earth, and to reflect that these elaborately constructed forms, so different from each other, are dependent on each other in so complex a manner, have all been produced by laws acting around us ...

There is grandeur in this view of life, with its several powers, having been originally breathed by the Creator into a few forms or into one; and that, whilst this planet has gone cycling on according to the fixed law of gravity, from so simple a beginning endless forms most beautiful and most wonderful have been, and are being, evolved.

— Charles Darwin, *On the Origin of Species by Means of Natural Selection, or the Preservation of Favoured Races in the Struggle for Life*

EUGENE BYRNE is a freelance journalist and novelist whose work focuses on history and has been published in many periodicals, including BBC History. *Darwin: A Graphic Biography* is the third historical graphic novel on which Byrne and illustrator Simon Gurr have collaborated.

SIMON GURR is a cartoonist and illustrator whose work for web, print and television is concerned with narrative and education.

ACKNOWLEDGMENTS

Robin Askew

Bristol's City Museum & Art Gallery

Bristol Cultural Development Partnership

Monique Brocklesby

Howard Brown

Lauren Byrne

Gareth Davies at Qube Design Associates

Down House

Alex Dunn

Christopher & Maureen Gurr

Julia Gurr

Dave Higgitt & Cath Evans at Venue

Brian Ireley

Rod Jones

Andrew Kelly

Mel Kelly

Paul J. McAuley

Jonathan Pomroy

Bob & Irene Pearce

Hélène Rattin

Amy Sanders

Sea Mills Library & Libraries West

Hans Sues

Vicky Washington

Wildscreen

And thanks to the many others
who have been so generous with
their time and help.

BIBLIOGRAPHY

WEBSITES

Leff, David. AboutDarwin.com. http://www.aboutdarwin.com.

Oxford University Press. *Oxford Dictionary of National Biography* online edition. http://www.oup.com/oxforddnb.

van Wyhe, John, ed. The Complete Work of Charles Darwin Online. http:// darwin-online.org.uk.

BOOKS

Darwin, Charles. *The Origin of Species.*
Oxford: Oxford University Press edition, 1996.

Darwin, Charles. *The Voyage of the Beagle.*
London: Wordsworth Classics edition, 1997.

Dawkins, Richard. *River out of Eden: A Darwinian View of Life.*
London: Weidenfeld & Nicholson, 1995.

Dawkins, Richard. *The Selfish Gene.* 2nd ed.
Oxford: Oxford Paperbacks, 1989.

Desmond, Adrian, and James Moore. *Darwin.*
London: Penguin Books 1992.

Kelly, Andrew, and Melanie Kelly, eds. *Darwin: For the Love of Science.*
Bristol, UK: Bristol Cultural Development Partnership, 2009.

Miller, Jonathan, and Borin van Loon. *Darwin for Beginners.*
Cambridge, UK: Icon Books, 1992.

Shubin, Neil. *Your Inner Fish: The Amazing Discovery of Our 375-Million-Year-Old Ancestor.* New York: Pantheon Books, 2008.

Stott, Rebecca. *Darwin's Ghosts: In Search of the First Evolutionists.*
London: Bloomsbury, 2012.

Thompson, Harry. *This Thing of Darkness.*
London: Headline Review, 2006. (Fiction)

Weiner, Jonathan. *The Beak of the Finch: Story of Evolution in Our Time.* New York: Vintage, 1994.

Zimmer, Carl. *Evolution: The Triumph of an Idea—from Darwin to DNA.*
London: William Heinemann, 2002.

This book may be purchased for educational, business, or sales
promotional use. For information, please write:
Special Markets Department
Smithsonian Books
P.O. Box 37012, MRC 513
Washington, DC 20013

Published by Smithsonian Books
Director: Carolyn Gleason
Production Editor: Christina Wiginton
Editorial Assistant: Danielle Villalovos
Cover Design: Mary Parsons

Library of Congress Control Number: 2012951786

ISBN 978-1-58834-352-9

Manufactured in the USA

17 16 15 14 13   5 4 3 2 1

For permission to reproduce illustrations appearing in this book,
please correspond directly with the authors.